LDS in the USA

LDS in the USA

Mormonism and the Making of American Culture

Lee Trepanier and Lynita K. Newswander

BAYLOR UNIVERSITY PRESS

Cover Design by Zeal Design Studio
Cover Image © Ashley Cooper/Corbis

Library of Congress Cataloging-in-Publication Data

Trepanier, Lee, 1972-
  LDS in the USA : Mormonism and the making of American culture /
Lee Trepanier and Lynita K. Newswander.
  176 p. cm.
  Includes bibliographical references (p. 143) and index.
  ISBN 978-1-60258-327-6 (pbk. : alk. paper)
  1. Church of Jesus Christ of Latter-day Saints--History.
  2. Mormon Church--United States. 3. United States--Church history.
I. Newswander, Lynita, 1982– II. Title.
  BX8611.T74 2012
  289.3'3209--dc23

                                        2011032169

BAYLOR
UNIVERSITY

Printed in the United States of America on acid-free paper with a mini-
mum of 30% pcw recycled content.

To our families and our spouses,
for their constant love and unfailing support
in all our endeavors.

CONTENTS

ACKNOWLEDGMENTS

Although our names are listed as the authors, this book is the culmination of the shared efforts of our families, friends, and colleagues. To all of these people we certainly want to extend thanks for their support, patience, and good graces while we worked to complete this book. We especially want to thank Carey Newman, who has been instrumental in this book from its inception to its completion, as well as the staff of Baylor University Press. Without Carey's and their assistance, this book would not only have been a much poorer product, but it would never have been published.

This book was a result of a chance meeting at Princeton University, where we were both participants at the Lehrman American Studies Center in the summer of 2009. Having learned about the Mormons from living in Utah for four years, Lee was looking for some project to explain his experiences with Mormon culture and its relationship to American civilization. Likewise, Lynita had just completed her dissertation on Mormonism in the Age of Jackson and had been searching for a venue to publish part of her findings.

Without the sponsorship of the Lehrman American Studies Center, we would never have met and therefore been able to write this book. To Mr. Lehrman and his staff, we want to express our gratitude for his invitation to Princeton, where this fortuitous encounter took place and resulted in this book.

On a final personal note, we would like to express our thanks and love to our spouses, MiJung and Chad, and Lynita's children, Madison and Lincoln. Without your unwavering support, this book would never have been realized. And although our names are on the cover of this book, you are the true coauthors of our lives. It is to you that this book is rightfully and most properly dedicated.

1

INTRODUCTION
For Another Thousand Years

The role of Mormonism in America has been simultaneously both exaggerated and undervalued. On the one hand, Mormons are seen with suspicion as part of a secret organization that seeks domination over the United States; on the other hand, they are marginalized and often excluded from national conversations about religion, culture, and politics in America. The fact is that neither account is accurate: Mormons have played a substantial role in the shaping of the social, cultural, political, and religious makeup of the United States, a role that is neither conspiratorial nor marginal and that has not been properly acknowledged in the academy or by the general public. This book is intended to remedy this deficiency. In it, we will explore the contributions Mormonism has made to American civilization and to the values that civilization claims to espouse.

When we speak of American civilization, we are attesting to those qualities that make the United States unique as a social, cultural, religious, and political entity. For example, the sociologist

Claude Fischer argues that community (family, church, job, and nation), abundance (material wealth, improved health, social opportunities, political freedoms, and self-mastery), and volunteerism (civic engagement) are at the core of the American character. The historian Arthur Schlesinger Sr. contends that the right to revolution, federalism, the consent of the governed, equality of women, the melting pot, freedom of worship, public education, voluntary giving, technology, and evolutionary progress are the characteristics of American civilization; while Harvard President Charles Eliot points to peacekeeping, religious tolerance, universal suffrage, the practice of political freedom, the welcoming of newcomers, and the diffusion of material abundance as the cornerstones of the American experience.[1]

The role of Mormonism in American civilization has been shaped by, as well as exposed the limits of, some of the values that Americans continue to espouse: religious tolerance, social pluralism, federalism, separation of church and state, the definition and importance of marriage, and Christianity. Mormons have been instrumental in representing and challenging these values in the realms of popular culture, the family, politics, and religion in the United States. As we will see, Mormons have not been completely accepted in mainstream American society. To a certain extent, the pattern of suspicion, accommodation, and eventual acceptance they have experienced is familiar to immigrant groups arriving in the United States, but what makes the Mormon experience unique is that they began within the United States and became outsiders within their own country. That is, the Mormons were forced to flee the United States—to become emigrants—before they became accommodated and accepted.

Before proceeding further, we should begin by defining Mormons and Mormonism. A Mormon is a practitioner of Mormonism, the largest branch of which is The Church of Latter-day Saints (LDS Church). The term itself is derived from the Book of Mormon, a sacred text to the Mormons that they consider to be a supplemental testament to the Bible. Compiled by the prophet Mormon and his son, Moroni, the last of his Nephite people, and published in 1830 by Joseph Smith, it recounts the tale of a fallen and lost indigenous American nation.[2] Although initially a derogatory nickname for members of LDS Church, "Mormon" became embraced by its followers. The term itself now not only refers to the religious aspect of these believers but also includes the social and cultural components that are associated with Mormonism.

The Mormons were forced to flee upstate New York to the Midwest and eventually to the West, where they established a theocratic state under the leadership of Brigham Young. As the U.S. federal government expanded its control westward, the Mormons became organized into the territory of and later state of Utah, where polygamy, separation of church and state, and federalism became contentious issues between the two parties. The tension between the Mormons and the federal government was such that an actual war, the Mormon War, broke out between the two groups.

When the Mormons decided to renounce the practice of polygamy, Utah was adopted as a state. However, they still were not fully accepted into the mainstream culture of the United States. Even today Mormons are often negatively portrayed in popular culture and are exposed to religious prejudice in the realms of politics and religion. This accommodation—but not acceptance—of Mormons raises questions about the faithfulness of the values to which Americans claim to adhere, such as religious tolerance and social pluralism.

In this book, we use the term "Mormons" to describe any believers who accept the Book of Mormon for their religious beliefs, while we use the term "Latter-day Saints" (LDS) to refer specifically to those who submit to the authority of the LDS Church headquartered in Salt Lake City. Besides the LDS Mormons, there exist the Missouri Mormons, who do not recognize the authority of the LDS Church, which include such organizations as the Community of Christ, the Church of Christ, and the Remnant Church of the Latter Day Saints, as well as the several polygamous practicing Mormon groups, such as the Church of Jesus Christ (Bickertonite), the Church of Jesus Christ of Latter Day Saints (Strangite), and the Fundamentalist Church of Jesus Christ of Latter-Day Saints (FLDS).[3] Here we focus mostly on the experience of LDS Mormons in America, with some references to the polygamous practicing Mormons as they have received recent attention in the media (for example, Warren Jeffs), and in popular culture (for example, *Big Love*).

Chapter 1 of this book looks at the positive and negative portrayals of Mormons in popular culture, such as in television, movies, and literature. In this chapter we see the limits of the American values of religious tolerance and the acceptance of social pluralism. As a vehicle of political organization, popular culture contributes to American democratic culture and its values, thereby transmitting Americans' reluctant acceptance of Mormons in their society. Although over time Mormons have been increasingly accepted into popular culture, that they are still regarded with suspicion reveals the limits of the values that Americans claim to hold.

Chapter 2 explores the questions of marriage, separation of church and state, and federalism in American civilization. When the Utah Territory applied for statehood, these subjects came to the forefront of the national conversation over the Mormon practice of plural marriage, more commonly known as polygamy, as questions were raised about the proper place of marriage, church-state relations, and the role of the federal government in the internal affairs of a state or territory. Although Mormons eventually renounced polygamy in order to obtain statehood, the role of Mormons in these subjects deserves another look.

Chapter 3 examines the obstacles that Mormon politicians contesting for national office face in having their religion accepted by mainstream voters. Again, this raises questions about the limits of religious tolerance in the United States and demonstrates the importance of religion in national politics. Although there is no constitutional or legal test about religion for national political office, there is a cultural one, and, because of their religion, Mormons clearly have not passed it. This chapter explores why this is the case.

Chapter 4 examines the theological beliefs of Mormonism and how these beliefs are not accepted by mainstream American Christians. The Book of Mormon, certain views on the afterlife, and the Mormon notion of a personal God are barriers for other Christians in being tolerant of Mormon theology. Mormons' strained relationship with other Christian denominations not only shows the limits of religious tolerance among religious groups themselves, but also points out the importance of Christianity and how it is defined in American civilization. We see that America is still a Christian nation, with Mormons asking about what constitutes the nature and essence of this Christianity.

The last chapter follows the contributions Mormons have made to the American narrative, and at the same time exposes the faults in that narrative. The American narrative, often adopted by immigrants to the United States, is one of the persecuted outsider who becomes eventually accepted socially and culturally as Americans, thereby exemplifying the virtues of religious tolerance, social pluralism, and separation of church and state. The Mormon experience is similar to that of these immigrant groups but also different in that, as noted above, the Mormons had to flee the United States before they became accepted and accommodated.

Because they challenge the values that Americans claim to cherish, Mormons have not been fully accepted socially and culturally in the United States. Thus, Mormons within American civilization simultaneously affirm and question the American narrative of tolerance, pluralism, and Christianity. Having its origins in America and ceding a special place to this country in its theology, Mormonism is, in many ways, the quintessential American religion. However, because some Mormon beliefs and practices challenge the values of American civilization, Mormons are regarded with suspicion and reservation by the American public. But it is through this very questioning of these core values that both Mormons and Americans define what American civilization is and will become.

This book is not a comprehensive account of Mormonism or a complete account of their contributions to American civilization; rather, it is an introduction for readers who know little about Mormonism and the role it has played in American life. Our thesis is that Mormon culture and the LDS religion embody certain tensions in American culture, and that they can be seen as simultaneously rejecting and reaffirming what are considered to be core American values. The history of the LDS Church and the politics and culture it has inspired are complex and involve not only multiple perspectives but also a considerable amount of criticism and debate. While this book does not ignore the most controversial issues regarding Mormonism and its beliefs and practices, it does not focus on those issues; instead, it is an introduction to major topics and key themes found in Mormon culture and theology. It connects popular culture, American history, politics, and social issues with what we contend is a distinctively American religion.

As an introductory text to the study of Mormonism, this book sits in good company. Richard Bushman's *Mormonism: A Very Short Introduction* provides a slightly different perspective on how the religion came about and what its basic theology, doctrines, and practices are. Like our book, it is written primarily for a non-Mormon audience, though it does not share the same focus on American culture and the relationship between the Mormon story and the American story. In that particular vein, our work approaches Harold Bloom's argument in *The American Religion* that Mormonism is a distinctively American religion in both its history and theology. Another complementary text is Armand Mauss's *The Angel and the Beehive*, which offers a critical analysis of Mormon culture as it alternately assimilates with and alienates itself from American culture throughout its history. The arguments in each of these books are foundational to those we make in this work; however, this text offers a unique focus on Mormonism's symbiotic relation to American culture.

Of course, there are several topics relevant to the study of Mormonism that this book is unable to address comprehensively. Richard Bushman's *Joseph Smith: A Rough Stone Rolling*, Fawn Brodie's *Joseph Smith: No Man Knows My History*, Jan Shipps' *Mormonism: The Story of a New Religious Tradition*, and the seven-volume *History of the Church*, written by Joseph Smith himself, are excellent resources for more information regarding the history of the LDS Church as both a religion and a social movement. Cultural studies of Mormonism and its position in more contemporary American society include Terryl Givens' *People of Paradox* and *The Viper on the Hearth*.

Other books on Mormonism in America are Richard Ostling and Joan Ostling's *Mormon America* and Claudia Lauper Bushman and Richard Bushman's *Mormons in America*. Theological discussions, including the seemingly inexhaustible debate regarding the place of the LDS Church as a Christian religion, are also abundant. Primary among them are Craig Blomberg and Stephen E. Robinson's *How Wide the Divide?*, Robinson's *Are Mormons Christian?*, and Robert L. Millet's *A Different Jesus?* and *Claiming Christ*. This is not an exhaustive list, but it does provide deeper levels of analysis into important facets of Mormonism that simply are not within the scope of this text.

We hope this book provides a balanced treatment of Mormons within the context of American civilization. Wanting to steer away from vehement apologetics and vitriolic attacks, we seek to acknowledge objectively the accomplishments as well as the miscues of Mormonism. We want to recognize the Mormon contributions that may have gone neglected, and to point out clearly the genuine differences between Mormon and American values. We do a service to neither party if we whitewash either the achievements or failures of both.

Perhaps the desire to be both distinct and American is a constant but ultimately irreconcilable one. In this sense, Mormons are no different than other ethnic, religious, or racial groups that have come to America with its promise of tolerance, pluralism, and prosperity. Yet today Mormons, because of their unassimilated status, still play their dual role as supporter and critic of the American project. But as Mormons have become more fully integrated into American culture and society, scholarship on Mormonism likewise has followed, and we believe this book continues this endeavor in being fair in its treatment, forthright on the controversies, and fresh in its approach. The answer to whether we completely succeed in this task, like that of whether the Mormons will become fully accepted in America, remains unknown.

1

MORMONS IN THE AMERICAN IMAGINATION

The Janus Face of Television

The portrayal of Mormons in American mainstream popular culture has followed two extremes: they are seen either as the epitome of all-American and wholesome values of family, clean living, and material success or as secretive, strange, and suspicious, with sacred temple rites, special garments, and a murky past that includes polygamy. The first set of values is personified in shows like 1970s *Donny & Marie*, while the second set is spelled out in the more recent show *Big Love*. These inconsistent portrayals of Mormons in the popular media may be entertaining, but they also confuse the reality and leave the public wondering what the true face of Mormonism really looks like.

In this sense, Mormons are both familiar and unfamiliar to the American public imagination. On the one hand, Mormons are the successful, helpful, and courteous neighbors that Americans want to have next door, while on the other they are the ones who have secretive temples and strange Bibles and talk in a coded language.

These disconcerting depictions are reflected in Mormons' own desire to be accepted by mainstream American society while at the same time adhering to beliefs and practices that run counter to it. This tension within Mormonism and in the popular portrayals of it embodies a tension within American popular culture: a simultaneous affirmation and critique of American values. By both asserting and questioning American values, Mormons have become a key voice in the ever-shifting conversation regarding just what it is that the American people stand for.

Donny and Marie Osmond were the first Mormons to break into American mainstream popular culture who were consistent with the all-American values of family, civility, and success. Donny emerged from the Osmond Brothers as a teen idol in the early 1970s with songs that became pop hits, such as "Go Away Little Girl" and "Puppy Love."[1] He and his sister, Marie, who was a country singer, had a variety show in 1976–79 called Donny & Marie that featured songs performed by the two. At that time, they were the youngest entertainers in television history to host their own variety show. When the show was canceled, Donny admitted that his public image was damaged because he was perceived by the public as "unhip" and as a "boy scout."[2] His clean-cut, all-American image was so damaging to his future career that one professional publicist even suggested that he should purposefully get arrested for drug possession in order to change it.[3]

Both Donny and Marie would have later success in their careers, although it never would reach the level of fame they achieved in the late 1970s. There would be other famous Mormon public figures—Gladys Knight, Steve Young, Johnny Miller—who offered differing portrayals of the LDS faith, some more positive than others. For most, acceptance would come at the cost of being connected with a conservative America. Those in popular culture who were secular and liberal would portray Mormons differently.

In fact, except for Donny and Marie Osmond, positive portrayals of Mormons in American popular culture are rare. A good example of negative representation is HBO's television series *Big Love*, which depicts a contemporary polygamist who lives in Salt Lake City with his three wives and seven children. Although the LDS Church renounced the practice of polygamy in the late nineteenth century, the family is described as Mormon,[4] leading the LDS Church to release an official statement about the show:

> The Church has long been concerned about the continued illegal practice of polygamy in some communities, and, in particular about persistent reports of emotional and physical child and wife abuse emanating from them. It will be regrettable if this program, by making polygamy the subject of entertainment, minimizes the seriousness of the problem . . . placing the series in Salt Lake City, the international headquarters of The Church of Jesus Christ of Latter-day Saints, is enough to blur the line between the modern Church and the program's subject matter, and to reinforce old and long-outdated stereotypes. . . . *Big Love*, like so much other television programming, is essentially lazy and indulgent entertainment that does nothing for our society and will never nourish great minds.[5]

In response, Carolyn Strauss, president of HBO Entertainment, stated, "It is interesting how many people are ignorant about the Mormon church and think that it [the LDS Church] actually does condone polygamy. So in an odd way, the show is sort of beneficial in drawing that distinction."[6] HBO also assured the LDS Church the show would not be about Mormons of the LDS Church. Whether such a distinction is made by viewers is unclear. However, both the LDS Church and HBO recognize the negative association in the American public mind between polygamy and Mormonism irrespective of the contemporary truth.

Big Love continued to create controversy when in 2009 the show recreated a temple ceremony, which Mormons consider sacred and therefore secret to non-Mormons. The creators justified their decision as being "a very important part of the story" and issued an apology in case they had offended anyone. As Mormon themes became more woven into the show, the LDS Church was placed in a difficult position. On the one hand, if it were to call for a boycott, unwanted media attention would be directed at the show and possibly raise Mormons' past association with polygamy. On the other hand, to ignore the show could be construed as condoning it. What the LDS Church opted for was to express continual disapproval of the show for being vulgar (rather than for being anti-Mormon) and to hope that the negative depictions of Mormons would not have any long-term harmful effect on the Church. It also suggested that individual members who were offended at the misrepresentation of the temple ceremony could boycott the show.[7] The LDS Church's response was similar to other religious organizations' reactions to negative portrayals of their beliefs and practices: issue a condemnation not on religious grounds but on grounds of poor taste, reaffirm the strength of one's organization, and encourage its members to protest it as Americans rather than as specific religious believers.

Other television shows like *Cold Case* and *Law and Order* also have represented Mormons poorly. In the *Cold Case* episode "Creatures of the Night," a serial killer, known as the "Mormon Kid," hears God in his head; his aunt dismisses the idea that he is crazy, saying, "Joseph Smith heard an avenging voice, so did Brigham Young."[8] The show also treats the Mormon sacred garments disrespectfully: they are referred to derogatorily as "gamies," and the protagonist fails to honor them properly. In spite of the warning that the show is fictional and does not depict any actual persons or events, the equation is clear: Mormons are strange people because of their beliefs and practices.

This same equation is also used in the *Law and Order* episode "Lost Boys," where (again with the warning that the show is fictional) the Mormon characters are portrayed as polygamists. Lighthearted but still insensitive to Mormons was *Boston Legal*'s running gag that one of the show's main characters will receive letters, presumably from angry viewers, when he mocks a female character by asking whether Mitt Romney ever wanted her for one of his wives.[9] In these and other fictional shows, Mormons are misrepresented as practicing polygamy and holding strange and bizarre beliefs. The all-American and wholesome values of Donny and Marie are discarded for the strange and sensational.

Interestingly, more balanced portrayals of Mormons have come in reality television series like *American Idol, The Real World, The Biggest Loser, America's Next Top Model, Dancing with the Stars, Survivor,* and others. Here Mormons are shown as friendly, courteous, and hardworking people who have beliefs and practices characteristic of conservative and religious America. An example of conservative values sticking out in a secular culture can be found on the show *Survivor,* where the participant Neleh Dennis brought her scriptures as her luxury item to the island and another participant, Ashlee Ashby, woke up at 5 o'clock in the morning every day to drive thirty minutes to church to study the Bible prior to the show.[10] In some parts of the country, these women would be viewed as role models; in others, they would be objects of ridicule. The clash between religious and secular values not only creates conflict on television, but it also reflects the political and cultural conversation that is taking place in the United States today. When Julie Stoffer in *The Real World* had to explain and justify her Mormon religion to her roommates, she became the central character of the series as the lone conservative and religious voice in a liberal and secular America.[11]

The advantage of having Mormons in reality television series is that they are able to represent an America that is both familiar and strange: conservative and religious but not well known or understood. As Julie Stoffer said, "One of the good things that will come out of this is that it's getting people talking about Mormonism. . . . If it takes a couple kids going on 'American Idol' to make that happen, well, damn it, good!"[12] This not only allows a natural conflict of religious and secular values, but it also invites a curious viewers to ask what constitutes Mormonism and, more broadly, what constitutes America.

The overrepresentation of Mormons in reality television series may strike some as extraordinary, especially given their history of persecution and oppression by their fellow Americans. Some have speculated that because Mormons come from large families, it makes them natural competitors in group dynamic situations, which are what reality television shows are based on. Others have suggested that their culture cultivates an openness and confidence that makes them attractive candidates on television. Finally, there are those who have pointed out that the Mormon practice of Family Home Evenings on Monday nights creates a natural built-in audience, especially when one of the contestants is "one of their own."[13]

But what may be more remarkable than the sizable number of Mormon contestants in reality television series is their acceptance by mainstream American popular culture and their ability to maintain their religious identity. Ken Jennings, who holds the longest winning streak on the U.S. syndicated game show *Jeopardy*, was so well received by mainstream popular culture that corporations like Microsoft, Cingular Wireless, and Allstate Insurance sought his public endorsement.[14] Jennings did not hide the fact that he was Mormon—he stated that he would donate some of his three million dollars in earnings to the LDS Church (as well as to National Public Radio)—but he did not make it the defining issue for his public persona.

Still, some in the mass media depicted Jennings as a Mormon, as opposed to a successful American. Jennings himself addressed this issue directly when he wrote an article in the *New York Daily News* asking the public to stop slandering his Mormon faith, especially in light of Massachusetts governor Mitt Romney's run for the 2008 Republican presidential nomination.[15] Thinking that his religion had been "effectively mainstreamed" ("Being a Mormon was like being Canadian, or a vegetarian, or a unicyclist," he said), Jennings was surprised to see the biased coverage Mormons received in the mass media, such as "Lawrence O'Donnell's bizarre anti-Mormon explosion on 'The McLaughlin Group'" or "Christopher

Hitchens, who called [his] church 'an officially racist organization.'" Finding himself, like many Mormons, a target of unfair stereotypes from the mainstream media, Jennings concluded with a plea for tolerance and civility, as well as a clarification of the LDS Church's positions on blacks and polygamy.

However, there are some portrayals of Mormons in mainstream American popular culture that are more positive, though not as traditional as the Donny and Marie model. For example, in the *South Park* episode "All about Mormons," the Mormon characters, particularly Joseph Smith Jr., are lampooned but in a good-natured manner, with the Mormon Harrison family depicted as polite, family-oriented, and successful. Although the story questions the religious origins of Mormonism, the Harrison family, particularly their children, are cast in a sympathetic light as victims of religious bigotry by the story's main characters. In another episode, "Super Best Friends," Joseph Smith, along with other religious founders like Buddha and Moses, joins forces with Jesus to fight David Blaine, a street magician who has superpowers. In fact, in the *South Park* world, it is only the Mormons who have predicted the afterlife correctly, with members of the other religions condemned to hell. Of all the characters portrayed in the series, it is only the Mormons who are consistently represented as "compassionate, or even courteous."[16]

Finally, there is the television series franchise *Battlestar Galactica*, which derives elements of its science fiction plot from the Mormon beliefs of its creator, Glen A. Larson.[17] For example, in both the 1978 and 2003 series, the planet Kobol is the ancient and far-away home world of humanity. In Mormon scripture, Kolob is a celestial body identified in the *Book of Abraham* (3:2) as being near the home of God.[18] Other instances of the Mormon influence infused into the series are the show's governing council, the Quorum of Twelve, which parallels the LDS Church's Quorum, and the characters' beliefs in marriage as eternal and in the gods as more perfected humans. Simply put, the show's plot—the search for a lost tribe and planet—and the religious beliefs that surround it, although placed in a science fiction world, are heavily borrowed from the beliefs of Mormonism.

In the 2003 series, the conflict between humanity and the Cylons is primarily theological, with the former as polytheists and the latter as monotheists. Although the Mormons consider themselves monotheists, they have been accused of actually being polytheists.[19] This monotheism-versus-polytheism debate is mirrored in the plot of *Battlestar Galactica*, where viewers' sympathy alternates between the humans and Cylons. Although Mormonism is not explicitly addressed in the television series, its influence is clear if one knows about the religion. By being woven into the fabric of the plot, Mormon beliefs resist both positive and negative portrayals, particularly in the 2003 series, where humanity and the Cylons ultimately cooperate with one another. In other words, the difficulty of assessing which group—the humans or the Cylons—is representative of Mormonism becomes less relevant as the plot progresses forward and the question of whether different religious groups can work together becomes more prominent.

Another ambiguous portrayal of Mormons appears in the HBO television miniseries *Angels in America*, adapted from a play by Tony Kushner. As *Battlestar Galactica* incorporated Mormon beliefs for the show's theology, *Angels in America* borrows from the Mormon understanding of history to structure its plot. Mormon characters are prominent in *Angels in America*, as are Mormon beliefs: the notion of prophecy, the sacred book and angels, and the conceptualization of history as millennial. Mormons understand time as a process of evolution and progress and hold out the possibility of unlimited growth, as do the angels in the play. Just as the early Mormons claimed an ideology of progress that was beyond the progress of Jacksonian democracy, the show advocates a utopianism that is beyond most contemporary ideologies of progress.[20] As the nineteenth-century Mormons were persecuted and forced to flee westward, so were homosexuals treated with prejudice and discrimination in the twentieth.[21] In both the show and in early Mormon history, the United States was understood as a place with a blessed past and a millennial future within a generation's grasp. Although the increasing visibility of Mormons in American popular culture could be interpreted as a sign of mainstream acceptance, one has to ask why the media so often, and stereotypically, make a point of a person's or a character's Mormon religion. Compared to other religious groups, Mormons are overwhelmingly a target of negative stereotypes, with their beliefs and practices considered strange rather than mainstream. Of course, there are exceptions to this representation of Mormons in mainstream popular culture, among whom one of the most recent and popular is Glenn Beck.

The Glenn Beck Exception

In 2009 *Fox News* gave an audience searching for "entertainment and enlightenment" precisely what it was looking for: a libertarian-conservative with strong personal and political values, a quick wit, and a take-no-prisoners attitude.[22] By this point, Glenn Beck already had a large and faithful following from his popular radio program and frequent appearances on CNN (where he had his own show from 2006 to 2008) and ABC's *Good Morning America*. But the marriage of Beck with the powerhouse conservative news network lent a new force to his message. Quickly, his program became number one in its time slot, which included the most sought-after demographics.[23] Millions of viewers tune in weeknights to see politicians, academics, and celebrities subjected to Beck's dogged determination to uncover truth to enlighten his viewers—a process that often includes considerable focus on his own sarcasm-laden commentary.

Further capitalizing on his media success, Beck is the author of four books that have reached number one on the *New York Times Best-Seller List*.[24] Despite their unabashedly narrow ideology and unapologetic critique of the political status quo, Beck's books have been incredibly popular. However, it is perhaps the warm-and-fuzzy short novel *The Christmas Sweater* (2008) that has inspired the most personal and hurtful criticism to its author. In anticipation of its success, the book was reviewed favorably by Focus on the Family, an evangelical Chistian non-profit organization which supports socially conservative public policy. The review, by guest reporter Karla Dial, highlights Beck's personal faith in Christ and the book's faith-promoting message of a young boy's struggle to learn the true meaning of Christmas. Shortly after its publication, Underground Apologetics, an evangelical Christian ministry headed by Steve McConkey, criticized Focus on the Family for promoting the writings of someone who was a member of a "false religion" and a "cult." According to the complaint, "while Glenn's social views are compatible with many Christian views, his beliefs in Mormonism are not."[25] Days later, Beck's interview was pulled from Focus on the Family's CitizenLink website.[26]

It is not that Beck has made much attempt to hide his faith. By his own design, Beck has spoken openly on his show about his journey of redemption and atonement, which included his personal struggles to overcome alcoholism and drug abuse. By preaching that personal values and political values ought to be one and the same, Beck has mastered an especially tricky balancing act that is not often rewarded in the popular media. It is this daring combination that keeps viewers tuned into his show. Still, to anyone who was not aware of Beck's Mormonism, it would seem that most of his principles are the same as those of mainstream conservative Christianity. His books sell well in evangelical Christian bookstores, and apart from the recent scandal regarding Focus on the Family, no real controversy has arisen regarding his faith.[27]

But whether his Mormonism is overt or not, Beck's unabashed infusion of religious values with political ideals has made a mark on the mainstream news media. His signature style of debate and commentary refuses to be ignored, and if ratings and book sales are any indication, millions of Americans are buying into his carefully crafted conservative-Christian-evangelical-Mormon message. And his peculiar ideology is making an impression: according to a 2009 Gallup poll, Americans consider Beck to be the fourth most-admired man alive. Positioned right between Nelson Mandela and Pope Benedict XVI (and also ahead of Billy Graham), Beck has worked his way into the esteem and won the acceptance of mainstream America in spite of his seemingly dangerous insistence on mixing politics with religion. What could be considered career suicide for many popular figures has proven to be a gold mine for Beck. His winning combination of arrogance and humility has gained him the trust and following of "real Americans."[28]

As some see it, Beck's unique style—and consequently his success—comes from his affiliation with the LDS Church. For example, many of Beck's core political values, such as an almost worshipful admiration of the American Founders and the Constitution, are deeply seated in LDS theology and did not appear in Beck's public persona until after his conversion to the religion in 1999. Furthermore, some argue that Beck's politics are inspired by the prominent Mormon (and staunchly conservative anticommunist) Cleon Skousen.[29] The result is that the politics of Mormonism are filling the minds and ballot boxes of America—perhaps unbeknownst to Americans themselves. As one columnist wrote, "Glenn Beck marks an unprecedented national mainstreaming of a peculiar strand of religious political conservatism rooted in, and once isolated to, the Mormon culture regions of the American West."[30] In other words, the political values advocated by Beck and his millions of followers across the nation are really the popular incarnation of Mormonism, born again into an easily digestible conservative form with a likable enough "pudgy, buzz-cut, weeping phenomenon" as its host.[31]

The mainstream acceptance of Glenn Beck is unusual, for the history of Mormons in American politics and the American political media has not always been so positive.[32] One might argue that the country is heading into a new era of acceptance of politico-religious grandstanding, thanks to Beck's success and that of the outspoken evangelical Mike Huckabee, with his own number one–rated news show.[33] Still, Beck is charting new territory as a widely influential Mormon thinker whose personal faith feeds into a unique political ideology that fuels a wide spectrum of American viewers and voters.

Mollywood

Though he may be the most outspoken, Glenn Beck is hardly the only Mormon to make waves in popular culture. Members of the LDS Church have also made their mark on the big screen in acting, producing, screenwriting, composing, and directing both in independent and blockbuster films. Whether their faith is mentioned publicly or not, the culture and values of Mormonism have a way of manifesting themselves in the media they create. In this way, the fabric of American culture continues to be influenced by LDS ideals that are accepted as unconsciously and heartily as movie popcorn.

The history of Mormons in the movies is as old as the genre itself. The first feature-length documentary was *One Hundred Years of Mormonism* (1913). Since that time, members of the LDS Church have become increasingly involved with moviemaking at every level. In fact, they have recently developed their own industry niche (lovingly dubbed "Mollywood"). Over the past decade, movies made for a Mormon audience have become a popular, lucrative, and critically acclaimed industry.[34] The movement began in earnest in 2000 with Richard Dutcher's *God's Army*, which chronicled the fictional lives of young LDS missionaries in Southern California.[35] Most of LDS cinema has dealt with LDS themes and appealed to a strictly Mormon audience, poking fun at the Mormon culture and religion in a self-deprecating manner. Although the production quality is generally low, the makers of these films can count on their audience for a steady stream of DVD sales. Among the few that have ventured into mainstream tastes are Dutcher's *Brigham City* (2001) and Ryan Little's *Saints and Soldiers* (2003), which garnered over a dozen best picture awards on the independent film circuit.[36] The filmmakers of Mormon cinema (made for Mormons, by Mormons, and about Mormons) see themselves as following the call of former Church President Spencer W. Kimball (1895–1985) who lamented once to a group at Brigham Young University (BYU) that "the full story of Mormonism has never yet been written nor painted nor sculpted nor spoken." He called on Church members to cultivate their talents and leave their inspired mark on the world.[37] While the Mollywood movement is arguably a step in the right direction, Mormon filmography as such has yet to reach out to a broader audience and have the impact on American culture that Kimball was hoping for.

This does not mean that there are no Mormons making mainstream movies, however. Many popular films have been written, produced, directed, or otherwise improved by the contributions of members of the LDS Church. In these films, there are no overtly religious overtones or other obvious indicators of LDS influence. But many do pick up on themes important to LDS values and way of life. For example, *Napoleon Dynamite* (2004), written and directed by Jared Hess, is full of subtle references to LDS culture, although its wide appeal made it a box-office smash.[38] Hess has gone on to direct larger projects such as *Nacho Libre* (2006), starring Jack Black, and *Gentlemen Broncos* (2009). Jon Heder, who played Dynamite in 2004, has found roles as an actor in such films as *The Benchwarmers* with David Spade, *School for Scoundrels* with Billy Bob Thornton (2006), *Blades of Glory* with Will Farrell (2007), and *When in Rome* with Kristen Bell (2010). Though Heder has not played a Mormon character in these films, he has brought to them a certain awkward, quirky, squeaky-clean sensibility that bespeaks the LDS culture in which he was raised. Heder has also spoken openly of his faith, telling late-night talk show host George Lopez on *Lopez Tonight* that he lives a straight-edge lifestyle, avoiding drugs, alcohol, and even caffeine.[39]

The influence of LDS values on mainstream movie culture is even more prevalent in animation. Don Bluth, a Mormon and graduate of BYU (like Hess and Heder), has directed, produced, or animated many of the most iconic animated films of the last century, including *Sleeping Beauty* (1959), *Oliver and Company*, *The Sword in the Stone* (1963), *Robin Hood* (1973), *Pete's Dragon* (1977), *The Rescuers* (1977), *The Fox and the Hound* (1981), *An American Tail* (1986), *The Land before Time* (1988), *All Dogs Go to Heaven* (1989), and many others. As one critic has mentioned, Bluth's LDS upbringing has thoroughly influenced his art, just as "Woody Allen's identity as a Jewish New Yorker is a driver of his comedy."[40]

Another popular animated classic that has an LDS influence is Disney's *Pinocchio* (1940), whose iconic, Academy Award–winning song "When You Wish upon a Star" was co-composed by Leigh Adrian Harline, who was a member of the Church. More recently, there is Edwin Catmull, a computer scientist who cofounded Pixar and is currently the president of Disney-Pixar animation. Catmull's position has led to an increased collaboration between BYU and the animated film industry. According to the *Deseret News*, his company hires three or four BYU graduates each year, and has numerous cooperative agreements with the university's animation and digital animation programs.[41] The efforts of each one of these individuals have, in some respect, brought LDS values of clean living and family togetherness to an accepting American audience. Through the guise of wholesome entertainment, these films have helped to make Mormon culture a large part of American movie culture.

Countless others have made their mark on the world of film in less predictable venues. For instance, LDS filmmakers produced *Schindler's List* (Jerry Molen) and *The Blair Witch Project* (Kevin J. Foxe). However, the overall Mormon impact on the movie industry remains inextricably connected with the same family friendly, G-rated values that define their culture. It is little wonder, then, that animation and quirky comedies have attracted the largest group of LDS film talent. It is through these sanguine and seemingly innocuous stories that the story of Mormonism, with its deep-seated, reverential belief in the American dream and values of family, sexual purity, and all-around clean living, enters the homes and psyche of millions of Americans and other viewers around the world.

Although overtly Mormon cinema holds little appeal for a mainstream audience, members of the LDS Church today are following the command given by their beloved prophet: to create the greatest art this world has ever seen. "It has been said that many of the great artists were perverts or moral degenerates," noted Kimball: "In spite of their immorality they became great and celebrated artists. What could be the result if discovery were made of equal talent in men who were clean and free from the vices, and thus entitled to revelations?"[42] The answer: "Our writers, our motion picture specialists, with the inspiration of heaven, should tomorrow be able to produce a masterpiece which would live forever." This is the call, and every day thousands of faithful and talented Latter-day Saints work to make it happen.

The Habits of Best-Selling Vampires

Much like the Mormon contributions to film and appearances in television, Mormon literature can be divided into two main categories: those which appeal to Church members, and those written for a more mainstream audience. In the first group are the novels with LDS characters and themes, and historical studies of Joseph Smith, Brigham Young, and the Church's pioneer heritage. These works are marketed heavily through Deseret Book, a publishing and bookselling company owned by the LDS Church.[43] Deseret Book supports the mission of the LDS Church "by providing scriptures, books, music, and other quality products that strengthen individuals, families, and our society."[44] Most of these works are by LDS authors, written for LDS audiences, although other religious merchandise and uplifting fiction and nonfiction are also available.

As a Church-owned company, Deseret Book cannot afford to let its standards slide. In 2009, "mixed review[s]" from customers led the bookseller to stop carrying Stephenie Meyer's *Twilight* series in its stores.[45] Though the books are still available through special order, the message is startlingly clear: even though Meyer is a Mormon and a graduate of BYU and her novels are best sellers, the appropriateness of their content is not unquestionable.

With all of her recent success, Meyer presents an interesting study of the LDS writer. A faithful member of the LDS Church, she decided to write for a mainstream audience, and the mainstream accepted her wholeheartedly. Until the publication of her first book, she was a typical stay-at-home mother of three. But all of that changed quickly when *Twilight* (2005) debuted at number five on the *New York Times Best-Seller List*. In 2008, *USA Today* recognized *Twilight* as the best-selling novel of the year.[46] Its sequels, *New Moon* (2006), *Eclipse* (2007), and *Breaking Dawn* (2008), were eagerly anticipated. The final installment sold 1.3 million copies within twenty-four hours of its release.[47] Thanks to the success of her books, Meyer was named one of *Time*'s 100 Most Influential People in 2008, and made a place for herself in *Forbes*' top 100 list of the most powerful celebrities.[48]

What is remarkable is that Meyers is able to accomplish success while maintaining the value system that she states is part of her identity: she does not smoke, drink, or watch R-rated movies, and her novels lack blood, gore, and sex. "I don't think my books are going to be really graphic or dark," she said in an interview with the *Times of London*, "because of who I am. There's always going to be a lot of light in my stories."[49] As a writer for *Time* noted, even though Meyer does not write about Mormons, "her beliefs are key to understanding her singular talent."[50] Meyer's work has become infamous for its "erotics of abstinence" and the author's singular ability to make what is "squeaky, geeky clean on the surface," such as hand-holding, long, lingering glances, and no sex before marriage, appeal to a mainstream audience.[51]

Meyer is not the only Mormon writer to gain popularity incorporating her religious morality into her fiction. Decades before *Twilight*, Orson Scott Card published *Ender's Game* (1985) and its sequel, *Speaker for the Dead* (1986), both of which won top awards for writing in science fiction.[52] One of Card's characters is a nonpracticing former Mormon, but there are otherwise no overt ties to his religion in the books. Still, Card admits that "Mormon beliefs and concerns crept into my work anyway, because I'm a believing Mormon and what seems true to me is always going to be more or less consonant with Mormon theology as I understand it and Mormon culture as I have experienced it."[53]

Another popular Mormon author who draws on his faith for inspiration is Stephen R. Covey, whose *Seven Habits of Highly Effective People* (1989) has sold over 15 million copies worldwide. Covey's explanation of what he calls "principle-based leadership" has continued to be one of the fifty best-selling titles at Amazon.com, even twenty years after its first publication. Thanks in part to this success, Covey has been named one of *Time's* 25 Most Influential Americans in 1996 and *Seven Habits* was named the number one most influential business book of the twentieth century.[54] Covey is also vicechairman and cofounder of FranklinCovey, which provides business professional services and organizational tools like day planners for individuals. Although Covey's widespread acceptance in both the business world and the lives of private individuals (his follow-up book, *The Seven Habits of Highly Effective Families*, first published in 1999, has also sold more than 1 million copies) has come from a seemingly secular set of principles, Covey has acknowledged that his religion inspires and influences his work. In fact, in *Divine Center* (1982), a religious book written for an LDS audience, Covey urged other Mormons to "testify of gospel principles" using vocabularies that would resonate with the "experience and frame of mind" of non-Mormons.[55] According to some, this is precisely what he does in *Seven Habits*: testifying of his personal religious values by secularizing them and thereby making them acceptable to the mainstream.

Admittedly, Mormon authors who write for the mainstream are few and far between. However, as these examples demonstrate, a number of them have reached success and touched millions of Americans who have been captivated by their winning combination of LDS values with fantastic stories or leadership strategies. Through their words, Mormon culture and values are introduced to an unwitting audience. And in many cases, that audience is more than willing to accept them. For its twentieth anniversary, FranklinCovey asked readers of its blog to share how *Seven Habits* had changed their lives. One respondent summed up the thoughts of dozens of other respondents by saying simply, "it changed everything."[56]

* * *

Speaking esoterically about one's faith—whether in television, movies, literature, or political ideology—has a firm foundation in the Mormon experience. Given their history of conflict, persecution, and exile, Mormons are justified in being wary when entering mainstream American society. They must balance making their religious beliefs accessible and familiar and not succumbing to secular values. To mainstream America, the message is that Mormons share the same conservative and religious values that other people do, while to Mormons, what is conveyed is that one's principles and beliefs are not compromised. For Mormons, this is a legitimate way to navigate a pluralist society in order to gain mainstream acceptance; for its critics, this is nothing more than equivocation and clever hedging. Whether this strategy will eventually succeed in gaining Mormons mainstream acceptance remains an open question.

This esoteric strategy is required because of the American public's unease with the perceived duality of Mormonism: its all-American and wholesome values and its seemingly strange and secretive practices. However, as religious minorities attain a certain size or significance, they become part of the mainstream culture and begin to be portrayed accurately in movies, television shows, literature, and the news media, though some stereotypes persist. The experience of the Mormons is no different in this respect. As Mormons have become more prevalent and open about their beliefs in mainstream American popular culture, anti-Mormon sentiment and expression have abated, promising a possible, more harmonious relationship between Mormon and mainstream culture.

In this sense, Mormons reveal inherent tensions in mainstream American popular culture. Americans seem to want the all-American values of *Donny & Marie* as well as the strange and the bizarre of *Big Love*. Mormons are ideal candidates for this dual role: they are a minority and are known but not well understood. They represent values that Americans admire, although their religion has historically been portrayed negatively. Thus, the portrayal of Mormons in the mainstream media as representing both exaggerated normalcy and oddity would seem to be a manifestation of American popular culture. That is, the political and cultural debates about liberal and secular against conservative and religious, the admiration for material success and clean living combined with a fascination for the strange and secretive, the affirmation of American values along with a constant critique of them constitute the essence of mainstream American popular culture, and these tensions have been manifested by various minority groups throughout America's history, of which Mormons are simply the latest. They make Americans aware not only of who these groups are but, more importantly, of themselves as Americans.

2

AN AMERICAN MARRIAGE

American Monogamy

The portrayals of the Mormon family in popular culture are schizophrenic: either a prosperous and proud, self-congratulatory nuclear family (like the Osmonds) or a secretive cult in which the husbands lead double lives of public monogamy and private polygamy (as in *Big Love*).[1] This dual representation reflects the complex history of marriage in Mormonism as well as the challenge that Mormonism has posed to the American conception of it. It is through this contestation of the American understanding of the family, and specifically its understanding of marriage as monogamous, that Mormons have made their significant contribution to American jurisprudence and revealed precisely how much they were willing to sacrifice to become the most "American" of the country's religions.

When the Mormons could no longer escape the jurisdiction of the federal government in Utah Territory, they applied for statehood, hoping that they would gain a measure of autonomy and the space to practice as they believed. In this process, the question of what constituted marriage became both a legal and cultural issue in the country. Traditionally, monogamous marriage in the United States was deemed not only divinely sanctioned but also a civilized practice and a natural right.[2] European political philosophers had long recognized that monogamous marriage benefited the social order in channeling sexual desire into the predictable procreation and care of children. The ethical virtues associated with monogamous marriage, such as consent, could also be translated into the political virtues of republicanism. For instance, in *Persian Letters*, the French Enlightenment thinker Montesquieu equated polygamy with despotism: the harem stood for tyrannical rule, political corruption, coercion, and selfishness, while monogamy stood for the opposite values, those necessary for republican government: moderation, liberty, and consent.[3]

These republican virtues associated with monogamous marriage were recognized in the early American republic. For example, the Anglican bishop William Paley's *Principles of Moral and Political Philosophy* (1785), which pointed out the benefits of monogamous marriage, became the most widely read college text on the subject of marriage in the first half of the nineteenth century. Paley's defense of monogamy was rooted in reference to God and focused on reducing fornication and other undesirable social practices. Compared to monogamy, polygamy did "not offer a single advantage" but rather produced the ills of jealousy, abasement of women, and abandonment of children.[4] The equation was simple: monogamy was equated with republicanism, with all its divine and social virtues, while polygamy was equated with despotism, with all its undesirable vices and practices. It was civilized, moral, and protected by law.

However, the federal government in the nineteenth century was not the recognized authority on the matter of marriage. The federal government lacked the specific regulatory power to implement its commitment to monogamy because marriage fell under the purview of the states. The Mormon practice of polygamy therefore brought the issues of federalism as well as the relationship between church and state to the surface. When Utah applied for statehood, the question of whether the federal government could regulate marriage could no longer be ignored. In all the previous applications for statehood, the federal government had never before dictated the standard of marriage for the prospective state.

The one area where the federal government did have direct authority and the means to implement monogamy was in its relations with the Native Americans. The principle of monogamous marriage was a significant aspect of the policy of Native American assimilation. The states themselves had established different standards for marriage (most of the differences regarded interracial marriages), but all of them adhered to the criterion of monogamy. Still, even after the passage of the Fourteenth Amendment and the 1866 Civil Rights Act, a single national standard did not exist for marriage until the controversy about the entry of Utah into the union.[5] The attempt to eradicate the Mormon practice of polygamy consequently was not only the first time the federal government played a direct role in defining marriage as monogamous, but it would also change the balance of power between the states and the federal government on social public policy, in favor of the latter.

For Time and All Eternity

Before examining the implications for federalism, it is worth looking at the central role that marriage and the family plays in Mormon theology and practice. According to Mormon theology, the family is not only an earthly good, but a divine and eternal one as well. As a result, the meaning of "family" for church members, today as it was in the nineteenth century, is both broader and more far-reaching than for most Americans. When husband and wife are married in Mormon temples, they are sealed together "for time and all eternity" instead of promising "until death do us part."

This belief that familial relations continue in the afterlife is a unique feature of Mormon theology that allows the family to be defined fluidly. Although the basic familial unit for members of the LDS Church today is a father, mother, and children, early Mormons, due to a revival of a peculiar doctrine, permitted room for more than one mother and a prodigious amount of offspring.[6] In many ways, the early Mormon practice of plural marriage (polygamy) can be seen as an experimental variation of already existing American values, in which the central tenets of loving, nurturing, and providing for one's family remained constant regardless of family size. In spite of being riddled with controversy, the doctrinal foundations of LDS theology provide some insight into how a community of American citizens could justify their departure from the cultural norm of monogamous marriage and the traditional nuclear family—and do so under the very American grounds of a millennial and literal reading of the Bible.

Although the practice of polygamy and early Mormonism as a system of belief may seem inseparable, this was not always the case. The Mormon Church did not begin to sanction polygamous marriage until 1843, more than a dozen years after its founding, and the revelation that sanctioned it took most Church members by surprise, including Church president Joseph Smith himself.[7] Polygamy was not a foundational doctrine of the Church, and even at its height was never practiced by more than a small minority of its followers. In fact, it was difficult for many members of the faith to understand and accept.[8] Many of Smith's most ardent followers left the Church and deemed him a fallen prophet because of it. Others, who were non-Mormons and guided by ulterior motives, became suddenly interested in Mormonism because of its seemingly open regard for intimate relations. Nevertheless, despite its less than wholehearted acceptance by the Mormon community itself, the reputation for polygamy and the scandal and outrage the practice attracted remain a part of the heritage of the Mormon Church and of nineteenth-century U.S. history.

The revelation sanctioning polygamy is canonized in Mormon scripture. It reads, in part, "if any man espouse a virgin, and desire to espouse another, and the first give her consent . . . then is he justified; he cannot commit adultery for they are given unto him. . . . And if he have ten virgins given unto him by this law, he cannot commit adultery, for they belong to him, and they are given unto him; therefore is he justified."[9] Joseph Smith shared the revelation with his followers and performed second, third, and additional marriages for many of them.

Although it was kept quiet, the doctrine of polygamy was controversial even among Smith's most faithful followers. Many members saw it as a test of their faith and took second or third wives only to show their willingness to obey God's commandments. Smith was mindful of the broad range of reactions evoked by the principle of polygamy and was himself overwhelmed by the weight of it. Even his wife, Emma, was upset by the doctrine. And understandably so: Smith took twelve secondary wives in the first six months of 1843. During the remainder of his life (which ended in June 1844), Smith publicly denied that he advocated or practiced polygamy, and only spoke of the doctrine with his most trusted friends. Still, rumors circulated regarding his relations with a growing number of women, and his reputation suffered. In conversation with family and other church leaders, Smith maintained that he was reluctantly following a commandment that he had undeniably been given from God, for if he did not believe that salvation was at stake, he would have rejected the practice himself.[10]

Mormons justified the practice of polygamy in part by invoking the ancient law of the Hebrew Bible, in which plural wives were a right of a husband who lived righteously and kept God's commandments. For example, Abraham took Hagar as a second wife in order to fulfill God's promise that his children would be numberless; and David was chastised for killing Uriah in order to have his wife, not for having concubines.

Smith and his followers believed that he had reintroduced the authentic Gospel of Jesus Christ to the world, and that in this "final dispensation," or the last stage of the earth's existence prior to Armageddon and the Second Coming of Christ, all things must be restored. This eschatologically driven belief meant that all the principles or practices that God had required of his people throughout earth's history would need to be accepted again. By embracing what they saw to be a full spectrum of early Hebraic and Christian traditions, Mormons believed that they were doing God's will. Polygamy was one of these traditions, and although it is no longer sanctioned by the LDS Church, the Church's members still believe that the period in the history of the Church when polygamy was practiced was necessary precisely because it was part of the restoration of all things.

The Mormon justification of polygamy also relies on the Church's own literal interpretation of the Bible. Literalist readings of biblical texts were common among nineteenth-century Christian sects in America, in part as a reaction against an influx of non-Protestant influences as a more diverse set of immigrants settled in the country.[11] The idea that an individual could read the Bible for himself and understand it as it was written was also democratic, because it essentially opened up the "secrets" of scripture to every man.[12] Conservative Christians and fundamentalists today continue to believe that the Earth was created by God in six days, that Noah saved humanity from a great flood that covered the entire planet, and that Jesus' miracles happened precisely as the Bible says. Mormons, however, were the only group to take upon themselves the distinctive call to resurrect the doctrine of polygamy as it was practiced by Old Testament prophets.

Furthermore, the early Mormon doctrine of polygamy and the celestial law of marriage that accompanied it fit seamlessly into a broader system of beliefs regarding the family unit as a spiritual entity espoused by the LDS Church. According to Mormon theology, men and women are the spirit sons and daughters of God, made in his image, and, as such, can approximate their relationship to him in their own family circles. Smith taught that families were a central part of life after death and that a person who lived a good life could live together with his or her family forever in heaven.[13] The Mormon idea of heaven is consequently largely dependent on the existence of the ideal family unit. Because familial ties, especially between husband and wife, are so sacred, polygamous marital relationships continue in the afterlife just as monogamous ones do.

Secondary to the historical and theological justifications for polygamy are practical explanations for its value.[14] Some argue that polygamy as practiced by early Mormons in the nineteenth century was defensible because it provided a sensible way for the Church to care for widows and other unmarried women. During the period when Mormons were moving west in great numbers, dependent women and children greatly outnumbered the men and therefore needed food, shelter, and care. Another practical benefit of polygamy was that it relieved the difficulty for a woman of managing her household by herself out on the frontier, where physical labor was required and life overall was hard. Apologists for polygamy during this period also argue that it was a blessing to women on the frontier who might not otherwise have had the opportunity for marriage or the right to own land and property. Finally, having multiple wives allowed a man to father dozens of children in some cases. The population boom that resulted was beneficial to the group as they worked to settle new land in the Utah Territory. More children meant that family farms could be more productive, and more residents made a stronger case for Mormon entitlement to the land.

A New Kind of Federalism

Whatever its justifications, the early Mormon practice of polygamy provided fodder for a bitter dispute between Church officials and the federal government. As a result of decades of troubles stemming from what neighbors perceived as Mormonism's peculiar system of beliefs, members felt they were not safe within the borders of the United States. When the Mormon pioneers set their sights westward and aimed for the Rocky Mountains, they were intent on leaving the country. Led by their new Church leader, Brigham Young, in 1847 the Mormons first settled in the Salt Lake Valley, which was still part of Mexico. The migration was a calculated political move by Young, who knew that the Mormons' conflicts with the U.S. government regarding polygamy would not easily be resolved. But when the Mexican-American War ended with the signing of the Treaty of Guadalupe Hidalgo on February 2, 1848, the United States had undisputed control of Texas and the territory that would make up the states of California, Nevada, and Utah. Any plans Young had to leave the United States and align the Mormons with Mexico or Great Britain were dashed.

Young quickly changed his plans. In the summer of 1849, just two years after their arrival, he and other members of the Mormon Church in Salt Lake City put together a constitution for the proposed state of Deseret. It was based on the constitution of the state of Iowa, where the Mormons had lived for a time before moving west. Young initially had intended to apply for territorial status, but when he learned that California and New Mexico were applying for statehood, he decided to follow suit. After all, statehood would allow the people a higher degree of sovereignty to handle their own affairs than would be available to them as a territory; and since marriage was a state rather than a federal matter, the possibility for the continuance of polygamy appeared to be genuine.

Unwilling to take the time to go through the usual channels, the citizens of Deseret opted to take their newly minted constitution directly to Washington, D.C., and hope for the best. The proposal was ambitious: the would-be state of Deseret encompassed much of the land the United States had just received from Mexico. It extended northward from Mexico to parts of the Oregon Territory, and eastward from the Pacific coast of Southern California to the Colorado River.[15] Had this proposal been accepted, Deseret would have included all of present-day Utah, most of Nevada, and parts of California, Idaho, Arizona, Colorado, New Mexico, Wyoming, and Oregon.

The federal government wasted no time in denying Young's ambitious proposal. Even without opposition from Mormon enemies who were enraged at the thought of a Mormon state in the union, the proposal would have failed because the territory that would be allotted to the state was too large, too unsettled, and simply too un-American at the time.[16] Furthermore, the proposed state did not meet standard qualifications for statehood, such as containing at least sixty thousand eligible voters.[17] Nearly a year after Young's initial petition for statehood, Congress officially organized the Utah Territory, shrinking its borders and secularizing its name.[18] President Fillmore, more concerned about the growing trouble with the Southern states, appointed Brigham Young as governor of the territory and generally allowed current Mormon political officials to stay in place.[19] Thus, the question of federalism—whether the U.S. government could regulate an area traditionally reserved to the states, in this case marriage—was postponed because the issue of slavery had become more pressing to the nation.

In 1856, after President Pierce allowed Young to continue as territorial governor, the people felt encouraged enough to put together a new constitution and proposal for statehood. However, they were disappointed again, this time with direct reference to the impending troubles between the North and South. Slavery was simply a more pressing concern to the federal government at the time. However, it is likely that Utah's application would have been rejected in any case. Concern about plural marriage became a national issue, with Republicans pledging at their 1856 national convention to do what they could "to prohibit in the territories those twin relics of barbarism, polygamy and slavery."[20] While the federal government was distracted by other matters, it could not allow such an important political battle to move to the forefront, and the issue was postponed.

The following year, U.S. relations with the Utah Territory continued to deteriorate. Soon after taking office, President Buchanan tried to remove Young as territorial governor because he believed that, as both president of the LDS Church and secular governor of the Utah Territory, he was incapable of fully separating the interests of church and state.[21] What makes this incident remarkable is the federal government's involvement in an issue that was then, prior to the Fourteenth Amendment, reserved for the states.[22] Like polygamy, the relationship between church and state became a federal matter rather than a state one. The federal government's relationship with its territories was thus drastically different than its relationship with the states; it treated its territories, at least the Utah Territory, as it treated the Native Americans: with direct control over social policies such as marriage and church-state relations.

The Morrill Anti-Bigamy Act also was representative of this new form of federalism. The act, directly targeted at the Utah Territory and the LDS Church, banned polygamy and limited church and nonprofit ownership to fifty thousand dollars in the U.S. territories. The latter stipulation was meant to curtail the growth of the LDS Church, whose assets were above the fifty-thousand-dollar limit. The federal government would have a direct say in the social policy of marriage and the economic policy of church-state relations. Although President Lincoln signed the act into law in 1862, no funds were allocated to enforce its stipulations. After the Civil War ended, the U.S. government could turn its attention more fully to the Utah Territory. In the years that followed, Mormon leaders were arrested and taken from their homes and families for practicing polygamy. LDS Church officers were forced to go into hiding to protect themselves, their families, and their assets. One of them, George Reynolds, who was arrested for his practice of polygamy, appealed to the Supreme Court, arguing that he was only following his religion and ought to be protected under the

Free Exercise Clause of the First Amendment. But the Court in *Reynolds v. United States* ruled against him, finding that the First Amendment did not protect religious practices that impaired the public interest.[23]

In 1887, through the Edmunds-Tucker Act, the LDS Church was disincorporated, and all funds and properties were seized by the federal government. In many ways, the Edmunds-Tucker Act finally gave teeth to the Morrill Anti-Bigamy Act by allowing federal backing for the appropriation of LDS holdings in excess of fifty thousand dollars.[24] In 1890, the U.S. Supreme Court upheld the Edmunds-Tucker Act in *The Late Corporation of the Church of Jesus Christ of Latter-day Saints v. United States*.[25] The result was a new kind of federalism, in which the U.S. government could now regulate marriage, which was traditionally a state issue, and religion, which was traditionally a matter of personal conscience.

It was clear from the Supreme Court's decisions, the Anti-Bigamy and Edmunds-Tucker Acts, the rejection of Utah's applications, as well as the arrest of Mormons and the seizure of their assets that the U.S. government and public were not ready to accept Mormonism as part of American civilization. The practice of polygamy and the functioning of secular leaders simultaneously as religious ones was too much for Americans to tolerate. The fact that Americans were willing to federalize these issues revealed how far they would go to prevent Mormonism from becoming American.

Under such pressures, it was only a matter of time before the LDS Church, in order to save its future, would feel compelled to make accommodations to the U.S. government. The Church would have to conform to American values to survive: it would have to renounce polygamy and accept separation of church and state in its political affairs. In other words, Mormonism would have to become a more "American" religion if its members wanted persecution from the U.S. government to cease.

In 1890 the renunciation of the practice of polygamy was declared by the fourth LDS Church president, Wilford Woodruff.

Having been given a new revelation from God, Woodruff spoke to Church members: "Inasmuch as laws have been enacted by Congress forbidding plural marriages, which laws have been pronounced constitutional by the court of last resort, I hereby declare my intention to submit to those laws, and to use my influence with the members of the Church over which I preside to have them do likewise. . . . And I now publicly declare that my advice to the Latter-day Saints is to refrain from contracting any marriage forbidden by the law of the land."[26] Encouraged by Woodruff's manifesto, Congress passed the Enabling Act in 1894, which set forth the steps that Utah would have to follow in order to meet requirements for statehood. Having won on the question of polygamy, the U.S. government had decided to accept Utah as a state.

But by this time, the territory was already changing rapidly from the insular Mormon community it had once been. The completion of the transcontinental railroad at Promontory Point had brought non-Mormons into Utah at an increased rate. With them came national political parties and varied schools of religious thought. With non-LDS business and families quickly filling the Utah Territory, along with federal legislation against the LDS Church and the Church's renunciation of polygamy, the threat of a powerful, completely Mormon state disappeared. As the U.S. map was quickly filling in around Utah, its statehood could not be put off much longer—at least not based on the old justification of its barbarity and disloyalty. In 1896, Utah officially became the forty-fifth state of the union.

The Irony of Polygamy

The battle over Utah's application to statehood seemed to resolve the issues of polygamy, church-state relations, and even the nature of federalism itself. By conceding to the U.S. government's demands, the LDS Church defined what constituted marriage in America as well as the proper arrangement between church and state. Thus, the LDS Church not only accepted this new kind of federalism, in which the U.S. government could intervene in areas traditionally reserved for the states, but it also became the American religion that delineated what values could and could not be accepted by American citizens.

Nonetheless, the LDS Church continues to be perceived in popular culture and the media as un-American, or at least as something of an oddity. The cause of this perception is not only the LDS Church's past practice of polygamy, but the continued existence of non-sanctioned Mormon polygamous communities. These communities, whether portrayed in popular culture like *Big Love* or in headline news about the Elizabeth Smart kidnapping, remind Americans of the divisiveness that Utah's application to statehood had aroused. Even though the LDS Church has repeatedly denounced the contemporary practice of polygamy, it cannot escape guilt by association. The irony is that the more the LDS Church aims to become "American" by rejecting polygamy, the more Americans, by looking to places such as polygamous communities, refuse to accept it. In short, the persistence of non-LDS polygamous communities continues to be one of the major obstacles to the LDS Church becoming fully accepted in America.

Even when both the U.S. government and the LDS Church punished practitioners of plural marriage, particularly between 1890 and 1929, polygamy persisted in some of the fundamentalist groups which had splintered from the LDS Church. The polygamists see themselves as the true heirs of Joseph Smith's teaching and cite fundamentalist leader Lorin Woolley's 1912 public statement about a visitation in 1866 by Joseph Smith and Jesus Christ to the polygamist John Taylor as evidence validating the principle of polygamy. Polygamist believers accepted Woolley's statement as revelation, and passed his teaching on to others. Thus the modern fundamentalist Mormon movement was born.[27]

From the 1930s to the 1950s, the fundamentalist movement gained increasingly public visibility with an established organizational structure, while at the same time it experienced permanent schisms and separations. Led by John Y. Barlow, the movement established itself in both Salt Lake City and Short Creek, an isolated town on the Utah-Arizona border.[28] Short Creek is of particular interest because in 1942 it established a tax-free cooperative association, the United Effort Plan, that implemented the nineteenth-century Mormon ideal of a unified community having ownership of the land, with everyone working cooperatively.[29] Although the LDS Church excommunicated fundamentalist members and encouraged people to report polygamist activities, and the Utah State Legislature passed a variety of criminal and civil laws against polygamy, the fundamentalist movement continued to grow.[30]

But the fundamentalist movement split into two factions over a dispute regarding Barlow's successor, Joseph Musser, who had become leader of the movement after Barlow's death in 1949. The dispute was between the Short Creek community and the Salt Lake City and Mexican communities. The Short Creek community disagreed with Musser's condemnation of underage and arranged marriage, which were practiced in Short Creek, as well as his appointment of his close friend and personal physician, Rulon C. Allred, as his successor.[31] The Short Creek community's rejection of Allred in 1954 formalized the schism between these two communities. The Short Creek community, which selected LeRoy Johnson as its leader, would eventually become known as the Fundamentalist Church of Jesus Christ of Latter-Day Saints (FLDS), while the Salt Lake City and Mexican communities, which accepted Allred, would become known as the Apostolic United Brethren (AUB).

But before the schism, both communities were galvanized by the 1953 Short Creek Raid. On July 26, 1953, Arizona state police officers and the Arizona National Guard arrested the entire Short Creek Community, which numbered about 400 members, including 236 children.[32] One hundred and fifty of the children were taken into custody and were not permitted to return to their parents for two years, and some parents never regained custody.[33]

Although the raid had the full support of the Arizona and Utah state governments and the implicit support of the LDS Church, it was characterized as "un-American" in the national media and compared to the government's brutal treatment of its Native Americans in the nineteenth century.[34] Under pressure from the media and lacking criminal statutes to enforce the antipolygamy clause of its constitution, Arizona released the parents and, after protracted legal battles over violations of due process, returned many of the children to their homes.[35]

For the LDS Church, which took steps toward becomings more American by permitting the U.S. government to dictate social policy to its members, the negative portrayal of the Short Creek Raid in the national media was ironic. The LDS Mormons believed if they rejected polygamy and separated church and state, their religion would be at least tolerated, if not accepted, in America. However, after the Short Creek Raid, it was the FLDS Church, in spite of its practice of polygamy and the fusion of church and state in its governing affairs, that elicited a national response in support of its community. Whereas the LDS Church continued to be viewed with suspicion by its fellow citizens, the FLDS Church was viewed with sympathy, even though it continued with the very beliefs and practices that had led Mormons to be perceived with hostility in the first place.

Since the raid, Utah and Arizona state governments have conducted only sporadic legal activities against Short Creek (renamed Colorado City in 1960) and other nearby polygamist communities. The community has grown to an estimated eight to ten thousand members, including its satellite communities in Salt Lake City and British Columbia, and still subscribes to the United Effort Plan, through which economic, educational, social, and political activity are controlled by the leadership of the fundamentalist church. The Church itself became formally established in 1991 as the FLDS Church. Until 2006, when FLDS leader Warren Jeffs was placed on the FBI's Ten Most Wanted List, an unspoken truce was followed by the FLDS on one side and the LDS Church, and the Arizona, Utah, and U.S. governments on the other.[36]

In 2004, Jeffs expelled a group of twenty men from Colorado City and reassigned their wives and children to other men in the community; and in 2005 he dedicated a new FLDS temple on the Yearning for Zion Ranch (YFZ), near Eldorado, Texas. The new temple received national media coverage in 2008 when 416 FLDS children and 138 women were taken into state custody after a call from a purportedly sixteen-year-old girl who reported abuse to Texas authorities. In contrast to the 1953 Short Creek Raid, the national media portrayed the FLDS Church negatively in the YFZ Raid. But after the call was traced to a woman unconnected with the FLDS Church, Rozita Swinton, who was known for filing false reports, and the courts had established that insufficient evidence of abuse existed to remove the women and children, they were returned. In 2008 the FLDS Church formally renounced underage marriage.[37]

Jeffs himself had returned to Colorado City and renounced his role as prophet of the FLDS Church in a conversation with his brother Nephi in 2007. Prior to this, he faced charges of sexual assault of minors in both Utah and Arizona. Jeffs was arrested in Nevada because his temporary license plate was not visible on his Cadillac Escalade and was extradited to Utah, where he was convicted on two counts of being an accomplice to rape in 2007. He was sentenced for ten years to life in Utah and was scheduled to face similar charges in Arizona but was transferred to a Las Vegas hospital for medical reasons. In the midst of these troubles, Jeffs resigned as the president of the FLDS effective November 20, 2007, and the FLDS Church's United Effort Plan, worth an estimated $100 million, was placed in the custody of the Utah court system.[38]

The difference in the media coverage of the YFZ Raid compared to the Short Creek Raid reveals the changing perceptions and acceptance of the LDS Church by Americans. By 2008, the LDS Church was able to distance itself from its past of polygamy and from the communities that persisted in that practice. It had become more fully integrated into American culture and society, so that the FLDS Church was now perceived as an oddity and the LDS Church as mainstream. Although an association still exists between polygamy and the LDS Church in the perception of the American public, it is not nearly as strong as it was during the period of the Short Creek Raid. The members of the FLDS Church are now seen as being as far from representative of mainstream Mormonism as David Koresh would be of Protestant Christianity.

Not attracting nearly as much national media attention but suffering from its own internal problems has been the Apostolic United Brethren (AUB), located in Salt Lake City and led by Allred. After the 1954 split, the AUB experienced growth, especially in the 1970s, when it gained new converts in partial reaction to the 1978 LDS revelation that permitted the admission of blacks to the LDS priesthood.[39] Under Allred's leadership, the AUB grew to about ten thousand members, with smaller communities throughout Utah and Colorado and even in Great Britain. However, Allred was assassinated in 1977 by members of the dissident LeBaron Group, whose family members believed that Ervil LeBaron was the true leader of Mormon fundamentalism.[40] Allred was succeeded by his brother Owen, and the AUB continued to grow in membership. Like the FLDS Church, the AUB maintains relations with civil authorities and the LDS Church where those parties disapprove but do not interfere.[41]

In the past decade, fundamentalist polygamy has entered the popular culture and been painted negatively by the national media. Besides the YFZ Raid, the 2002 abduction of Elizabeth Smart by the polygamist Brian Mitchell (who is not representative of polygamist groups) and Wanda Barzee sparked a national media frenzy, especially after Elizabeth's return to her family in 2003. The press and television shows like *America's Most Wanted, Dateline, The Today Show, The Nancy Grace Show,* and *The Oprah Winfrey Show* have uniformly portrayed polygamy as practiced by fundamentalists in a negative light.[42] Interestingly, Winfrey herself was not disparaging of polygamist families who lived more mainstream lives in suburban centers across the United States.[43] Still, disapproving depictions of fundamentalist polygamy persist in the national popular culture, with books like *Under the Banner of Heaven* (2003) and *Stolen Innocence* (2008) and films like *The Elizabeth Smart Story* (2003) and *Banking on Heaven* (2006) depicting polygamy as harmful and destructive to marriage and the family.[44]

But perhaps the television show *Big Love* (2006–11) has introduced polygamy to mainstream popular culture like no other event. Polygamy in *Big Love* has been cast in a sympathetic or at least neutral light. The leading characters are compelled to lead a double life in their monogamous and polygamous worlds, thereby generating audience sympathy for the Henrickson family as outsiders. Television critics of *Big Love* have for the most part interpreted the polygamous lifestyle as a literary device rather than debating the moral and legal merits of the practice.[45] However, the LDS Church has criticized the show for its depiction of polygamy.[46] The Church's underlying concern is clear: it fears that the public will associate the practice of polygamy with mainstream Mormonism as it once had. Whether this will occur remains to be seen.

* * *

The continued existence of the fundamentalist communities poses a threat to the LDS Church as an American institution. Although it has renounced polygamy, the LDS Church still is associated with the practice, all the more so when references to polygamy are made in the national media and culture. This would explain the LDS Church's strategy of alternate silent disapproval and explicit condemnation of the FLDS, AUB, and other polygamous communities. If the polygamous communities do not enter into the public consciousness, then it is better to remain quiet about them so that people do not remember the "un-American" origins of the LDS

Church. But if the polygamous communities receive attention in the national media and culture, then it is incumbent upon the LDS Church to remind the public that it is committed to the American institution of monogamous marriage between a man and a woman. Public service announcements and ads on radio, TV, and the Internet with the slogan "Family: it's about time" are examples of the many strategies for improving the public perception of the LDS Church as an institution fully in concert with American values.

This desire to separate itself from Mormon fundamentalism and align itself more closely with the American mainstream may also partially explain what appears at first contradictory political behavior by Mormons on the same-sex marriage question. On the one hand, the LDS Church officially condemns homosexual behavior and supported, for example, Proposition 8, the California constitutional amendment that recognizes marriage as between one man and one woman.[47] On the other hand, the LDS Church endorsed Salt Lake City's nondiscriminatory ordinance in housing and the workplace against sexual orientation.[48] These two seemingly contradictory positions are reconciled when one considers not only the theological position of the LDS Church but its place in American culture and civilization. First, the LDS Church condemns only homosexual behavior and not homosexuality itself; consequently, one can be a devoted believer and also a homosexual, according to LDS beliefs. Discrimination in housing and the work place against such a person therefore would be difficult to justify. Second, the LDS Church paid an enormous price to enter into American civilization by renouncing the practice of polygamy in favor of monogamous marriage between one man and one woman. To give up this position for same-sex marriage would be an affront to those ancestors who made that sacrifice.[49] Recent statements made by LDS Church leaders that "marriage between a man and a woman is ordained of God and that the family is central to the Creator's plan for the eternal destiny of His children" affirm this position.[50]

As the LDS Church has entered into mainstream American culture, America likewise has become shaped by the LDS Church: the questions of marriage, separation of church and state, and federalism have been clarified by the debate over Utah's entrance into the union; the growing acceptance of the LDS Church, as demonstrated in the differing national reactions to the Short Creek and YFZ Raids; and the current debate over same-sex marriage, where the LDS Church plays an active role in determining the future of this social institution for our country. In many ways, the LDS Church is *the* American religion because it has challenged American conceptions of marriage, family, and government and then subsequently accepted and promoted them. We may have thought these issues were resolved long ago, but it is only when we examine the role of Mormonism in the history of our country that we see that our conceptions of them have been significantly shaped by the Mormons.

3

THE POLITICAL KINGDOM OF GOD

The Core American Values

As Mitt Romney ran for the 2008 Republican nomination for the presidency, Damon Linker of the *New Republic* and Richard Lyman Bushman of Columbia University conducted a provocative exchange about whether the American public has anything to fear from a Mormon president. Linker described the fundamental difference between Mormonism and mainstream Christianity as lying in the Mormons' belief about the vital role that the United States will play during the end times and the central place of prophecy in their religion, which precludes the possibility of philosophical reason to check its revelations.[1] As previously the fear had existed that a Catholic president would take orders from the Vatican, some in the American public are concerned that a Mormon president would follow Church authorities or rely on his or her faith inappropriately when making political decisions. Although Linker admitted that the Constitution does not require a religious test for qualification to political office, he does believe it is appropriate to ask Mitt Romney about his religious faith because Mormonism, like Islam, is a binary religion where one must accept everything or nothing. Unlike Judaism, Protestantism, or post–Vatican II Catholicism, Mormonism lacks a liberal tradition, so that Mormons envision their faith not as a repository of moral wisdom but as one of absolute truth. Mitt Romney as president would thus have to choose whether he was first an American citizen or a Mormon believer.

Bushman defended Mormonism by noting that prophecy in the LDS Church is constrained by "the moral law [that] is enunciated endlessly in Mormon scriptures. The Ten Commandments were rehearsed in an early revelation, reinstalling them as fundamentals of the Church."[2] New revelations would not be able to call for acts of violence if so prophesied, since they would be restrained by previous revelations that are considered fundamental to the LDS Church's theology. According to Bushman, the fact that prophecy operates within the framework of this older revelation is an adequate safeguard for preventing its abuse. It is analogous to how the Supreme Court decides cases within the framework of the Constitution: the prophet's authority depends on reasoning from past revelations as well as from all past decisions.

For Linker, past revelations are not an adequate safeguard for subsequent revelations: the lack of a natural law tradition or other theological resources other than revelation to moderate future prophecy is a serious concern for him.[3] In response, Bushman reiterated his earlier point that the historical evidence of the Mormon past does not give credence to Linker's concerns. Although Bushman admitted this concern, "rooted as it is in logic rather than reality," is a theoretical possibility, he believes that at the heart of this debate is the fear of Mormons commandeering "the United States government to advance their cause"—a fear that is fundamentally irrational and can never be alleviated no matter what Mormons do.[4] It is this fear that is the prominent obstacle in the quest for the presidency by Mormon politicians.

In the United States, it is taught that allegiance to the Constitution trumps ethnic differences, language barriers, and religious
beliefs. The newest arrival to the United States is no less American than the great grandson or granddaughter of the Pilgrims or
the Founders. This acceptance of all people with their different
customs, practices, and beliefs reflects some of the core values of
American civilization: religious tolerance, respect for social pluralism, and separation of church and state. These values are not only
codified in the Constitution and the laws of this country, but are
also part of a mythology in which citizens believe that anyone can
become president of the United States.

The apprehension of the American public about a Mormon
president, like the Mormon experience in the past, demonstrates
not only the difficulty of American civilization in accepting Mormons, but also the limits of these American values. For much of the
nineteenth century, Mormons in America were unassimilated—
the "religious other." Before entering the union, they had fled the
United States due to persecution, fought a war against the U.S.
army, and been denied statehood twice. Their religious beliefs and
practices—from continuing revelation to polygamy—seemed to
many Americans superstitious and barbarous. And most worri-
some, Mormons were seen as discriminating against other religious
groups in their state while fusing their own religious and political
authorities together.

Although some of these accusations were objectively not true,
such as discrimination against nonmembers or religious intolerance, these indictments would stay with Mormon public figures,
and to their detriment. This is particularly true of national politicians, for whom even today their religion becomes a central issue
in the national media. The irony is that the suspicions that the
American public continues to have about Mormons—about their
intolerance, their social homogeneity, their religion of continuing
revelation—actually reflect the religious intolerance and lack of
respect for social pluralism in the United States. That is, Americans

project their own fears and prejudices upon a religious group about which they know little. Americans' own intolerance and desire for cultural conformity do not come under self-examination but are directed against a group that wants to be accepted but continues not to be.

Thus, the core values of American civilization are applied to every ethnic and religious group in the United States except Mormons and Muslims.[5] This is most evident in the reception of Mormon politicians who have run for the presidency, but it is also noticeable even with Mormon politicians who do not aspire to the White House. Even though Mormons have made strides in becoming more accepted by the national political class, when making political decisions, they continue to face obstacles as a result of their faith. These obstacles, in turn, reveal the value and the limits of religious tolerance and the respect for social pluralism in the United States.

Joseph Smith: An Independent Man with American Principles

The first Mormon to vie for the presidency was Joseph Smith. Advocating a return to the "holy principles of '76," Smith ran as an independent candidate in 1844. The thirty-eight-year old ran on a platform that sought compensation for the Mormons' losses in life and property when they were expelled from Missouri as well as the promotion of religious rights, the purchase of freedom for slaves, and the overhauling of the economy in the populist mode.[6] His supporters established a political newspaper in New York City that described him as "neither a Whig, a Democrat, or pseudo democratic President, but a President of the United States, not a Southern man with Northern principles, or a Northern man with Southern principles, but an independent man with American principles."[7]

Besides being the founder and leader of the Mormon Church, Joseph Smith was mayor of Nauvoo, Illinois, a community second only to Chicago in population in the state.[8] A nominating convention held in the spring of 1844 believed that Smith could carry between two hundred thousand and five hundred thousand votes (15 percent of the American electorate) and that, although he would not win the presidency, he would be able to determine the outcome of the election.[9] Confident of this prospect, four hundred political missionaries departed from Nauvoo to proselytize Mormonism and promote Smith's bid for the presidency.[10]

Privately, Smith prophesied the collapse of the U.S. government within his own lifetime, to be replaced by his political kingdom of God in fulfillment of the Old Testament prophecy: a divinely inspired theocratic democracy would be established as the new government for the United States.[11] However, Smith's candidacy was eclipsed by the crisis of Nauvoo, where anti-Mormon sentiment forced Smith to disarm his militia and flee to Iowa. When Illinois governor Thomas Ford promised his safety, Smith agreed to return to face charges in Carthage. He was jailed there on June 24, and three days later was assassinated by a mob.[12]

Although Joseph Smith could potentially have had an effect on the 1844 presidential election, his candidacy was doomed by religious prejudice and violence. For him and his followers, his platform to run as "an independent man with American principles" was an attempt to be accepted into American civilization. The claim that he was the most American of all the candidates —neither Northern nor Southern—was an assertion that he and his religion were truly American. Winning, or at least influencing who would win the White House, would be the ultimate symbol that Mormons were truly Americans.

But when this hope of acceptance was destroyed by Smith's assassination, the Mormons had to travel to the West to create a separate community apart from the United States. Although there was religious prejudice against other groups, such as Catholics and Jews, during the nineteenth century, only the Mormons had to flee the country in order to survive. Smith's candidacy therefore epitomizes the religious prejudice and violence that Mormons had to confront in nineteenth-century America. Religious tolerance and respect for social pluralism would not be extended to them. It would take more than a century for another Mormon to run for the presidency, in the hope this intolerance against them no longer existed in America.

Brainwashed in the 1960s: George Romney

After the contentious admission of Utah into the union, Mormons became accepted and partially assimilated into American civilization. They became successful in politics at the state and national level, and, in 1968, a Mormon, George Romney, sought the Republican nomination for the White House. In 1844, Mormons were considered outcasts and ultimately persecuted in the United States. But the 1968 presidential election year could be characterized as one of religious tolerance and respect for Mormons. Americans had come to accept Mormons as American citizens in a period where an ideology of religious tolerance was predominant among the political elite, and religion, after John F. Kennedy's election to the presidency in 1960, played little role in the public mind. Capturing the White House would accomplish for Mormons what Kennedy's election had done for Catholics: symbolize the ultimate acceptance of his faith by his fellow American citizens.

Romney had been the chairman of the American Motors Corporation (1954–62) and the governor of Michigan (1963–69). With both Governor Nelson Rockefeller of New York and Governor William Scranton of Pennsylvania not wanting to run, Romney became the frontrunner for the nomination; a Gallup poll in November 1966 had him leading former vice president Richard Nixon by 39 percent to 31 percent in November 1966, and a Harris poll had him leading President Johnson by 54 percent to 46 percent.[13] But on February 28, 1968, with national polls projecting him to lose to Nixon in the New Hampshire primary on March

12—the very first of the contest—by a six-to-one margin, Romney announced his withdrawal from the presidential campaign.[14] The news shocked the political world, as most people thought he would run at least in the New Hampshire and Wisconsin primaries.[15] At the 1968 Republican National Convention, Romney neither released his delegates nor campaigned for the nomination. He lost to Nixon for the nomination with the vote 1,119 for Nixon and 186 for Romney. But after the Republican convention, Romney worked to support Nixon in the general election.[16]

There are several theories as to why Romney—a successful governor of an important state with the air and appearance of a president—lost the Republican nomination. For Romney, it was Rockefeller's lukewarm public support and willingness to enter into the campaign that were the chief causes.[17] After the polls showed Nixon well ahead of Romney before the New Hampshire primary, Rockefeller continued to support Romney publicly, although mentioning he would be available to run against Nixon if asked. In essence, Rockefeller did not want to appear to betray his pledge to support Romney but he was willing to do so by offering his services to campaign against Nixon for the Republican nomination. In addition to Rockefeller's tepid support for Romney, other factors that hurt Romney's run for the nomination were a badly managed campaign that was beset by internal rivalries, poor publicity from the 1967 Detroit riots, and a gaffe-prone public persona.[18] Exemplifying the internal problems in his campaign is Romney's infamous "brainwashing" remarks, which led to serious questions about his competence to be president.

On August 31, 1967, in a taped interview in Detroit, Romney made an offhand and unplanned remark at the end of a long day of campaigning. Initially he had supported the Vietnam War, calling it "morally right and necessary."[19] Now he favored peace as soon as possible: "When I came back from Viet Nam [in November 1965], I'd just had the greatest brainwashing that anybody can get. . . . I no longer believe that it was necessary for us to get involved in

South Vietnam to stop Communist aggression in Southeast Asia."[20] The "brainwashing" remark, as it became known, reappeared in the *New York Times*, and eight other governors who had accompanied Romney on the 1965 trip criticized Romney's comments as "outrageous, kind of stinking. . . . Either he's a most naïve man or he lacks judgment."[21] Romney's comments were used by his opponents to make him appear feeble-minded, as if he had accepted the "brainwashing," and played into the American public's fears of prisoners of war who were brainwashed and would act against their country, as portrayed in the 1962 film, *The Manchurian Candidate.* The comments were devastating to Romney's campaign, with his ratings dropping from 11 percent behind Nixon to 26.[22]

Whether Rockefeller's willingness to run against Nixon, the "brainwashing" remark, or the internal problems within his own campaign led to Romney's failure to secure the Republican nomination is an open question. What is of interest is that religion appeared to play no role in Romney's defeat and very little in his entire presidential campaign.[23] Part of this may be due to a president's religious faith having become a less important factor after Kennedy's election. Another factor may be that the tumultuous events of the time—the Vietnam War, the Civil Rights Movement, and the culture wars—overshadowed concerns about religious qualifications for the presidency. Finally, this was a period when an ideology of religious tolerance was at its apex, before the time when conservative religious voters became socially and politically engaged. This is demonstrated by the fact that the liberal, secular wing of the Republican Party (Romney belonged to the latter) seriously vied for the presidential nomination.[24]

The only time when George Romney's Mormon faith became an issue was when the LDS Church's doctrine commonly known as "the Curse of Cain," which denied African Americans the prestigious position of the priesthood in the Church, was mentioned. This doctrine would not be rejected by the LDS Church until 1978, but posed no serious problem for Romney because of his strong pro-civil rights record as governor of Michigan. Romney himself credited his poor background and subsequent life experiences with giving him a perspective on race relations that differed from that of the LDS Church: "It was only after I got to Detroit that I got to know Negroes and began to evaluate them and I began to recognize that some Negroes are better and more capable than lots of whites."[25] In his first State of the State address, Romney declared that "Michigan's most urgent human rights problem is racial discrimination," and he created the state's first civil rights commission.[26] One of the first to praise the awarding of the Nobel Peace Prize to Martin Luther King, he personally led a civil rights march in Detroit in 1965.[27] Romney also strongly disagreed with the conservative wing of the Republican Party, especially on civil rights, stating, "Whites and Negroes, in my opinion, have *got* to learn to know each other. Barry Goldwater didn't have any background to understand this."[28] Although the 1967 Detroit riots damaged his reputation, Romney's governorship made strong gains in civil rights relating to public employment, government contracting, and access to public accommodations.[29]

As governor, George Romney was also successful in overhauling the Michigan tax code and increasing state spending on education, local government, and welfare, with bipartisan support.[30] But the political strategy that had worked so well in Michigan—being an independent who operated outside traditional partisan politics and kept a distance from Republican organizational elements—could not be translated onto the national stage.[31] After Nixon won the presidency, Romney was named Secretary of Housing and Urban Development (1969–73) and soon after proposed an Open Communities policy in which local communities would be deprived of federal funding until they ended racial discrimination.[32] This plan would eventually fail after the U.S. attorney general, John Mitchell, refused to intervene.[33] Another policy proposal that was rejected by the White House was to increase housing for the poor to spearhead desegregation.[34] The blocking of these and other initiatives by the White House led Romney to resign his position after Nixon's re-election.

After his life in politics, Romney became a founding chair of the National Volunteer Center, which promoted volunteerism, and served as patriarch of the Bloomfield Hills Stake for the LDS Church.[35] He would briefly return to the public eye in two Senate campaigns in 1994. When his son, Mitt, ran for a Massachusetts Senate seat against Edward Kennedy in 1994, George Romney took an active role as a surrogate in fundraising events. When the Kennedy campaign made an issue of the LDS Church's past policy on African Americans, George Romney stated, "I think it is absolutely wrong to keep hammering on the religious issues. And what Ted is trying to do is bring it into the picture."[36] In a Senate campaign in Michigan, Ronna Romney, George's ex-daughter-in-law, sought the Republican nomination. However, George already had endorsed the eventual winner, Spencer Abraham, before Ronna announced her bid.[37] George continued to endorse Abraham but did not personally campaign for him. After both Romneys lost in 1994, George returned to private life and died of a heart attack at the age of eighty-eight the following year.[38]

Family Business: Mitt Romney

While George Romney, unlike Joseph Smith, did not confront outright hostility in his bid for the presidency, Mitt Romney would be challenged by a returning suspicion about his religious faith by his fellow citizens. In the 1990s and 2000s, a politician's religion again became a legitimate topic of debate, especially among the Republican Party as its members became more religious and conservative.[39] This raised questions of religious tolerance, respect for social pluralism, and church-state relations, and, for Mormons, brought to the forefront the question of whether they are considered fully assimilated citizens of the United States.

Mitt Romney first found his religion to be a political liability when he challenged Edward Kennedy for the Senate in 1994.

Although he was slightly leading Kennedy in the polls in September, in the end he lost 41 percent to 58 percent.[40] One of the great ironies of the campaign is that while Kennedy's brother, John, had to overcome the American public's religious prejudice against Catholics to win the presidency in 1960, the Kennedy camp initially used Romney's Mormon faith against him. Kennedy and his workers seemed to have forgotten then-Senator John F. Kennedy's famous 1960 pledge that his own Catholicism would not inform his constitutional obligations as president.[41] The irony was not lost on the media or the Romney campaign, which quickly made an issue out of it. The Kennedy camp, finding that the tactic was not having the desired effect on the electorate and was leaving them exposed to accusations of hypocrisy and religious bigotry, backed away from making Romney's Mormon faith a political issue.

More successful were accusations that Romney had cut workers' pay and benefits when he was CEO of Bain Capital and that he was a political opportunist, as shown by his shifting political views on abortion.[42] By early October, Kennedy was ahead by 49 percent to 44 percent. In their first televised debate, Kennedy was able to persuade the voters that "the Kennedys are not in public service to make money. We have paid too high a price in our commitment to the public service of this country."[43] This appeal seems to have clinched the election for Kennedy, and Mitt Romney lost his first bid for national office.

Following his Senate loss, Romney assumed leadership of the Salt Lake City Olympic Committee (SLOC) after it had been accused of bribery of top officials. He was successful in reforming the SLOC, connecting it with the local community, and overseeing a safe and profitable 2002 Winter Olympic Games. His motivation for taking over the SLOC was a combination of looking for a new challenge and being concerned about the reputation of the LDS Church suffering from being associated with a tainted Olympic Games.[44] Interestingly, what surprised Romney the most was the religious issue: "I would never have guessed that a religion would be such a big matter for the Olympics. I grew up in Michigan; I was the only Mormon in my school. Ann and I had lived in Massachusetts for thirty years where members of my faith made up less than a half a percent of the population. Where I had lived, church affiliation wasn't an issue."[45] The religious issue was the SLOC's need to have the LDS Church's support, particularly a five million dollar request as well as use of some of church property for the Olympics, while at the same time not alienating the broader non-Mormon community of Salt Lake City.[46]

While Romney's faith had played a role in his public life, such as in the 1994 Senate campaign, it never became the defining issue of his public persona until this moment. With the Olympics hosted by Salt Lake City, Romney had to directly confront the Mormon matter. First, when the national press portrayed the Olympics as "the we're-not-weird Games" and "the Mormon Games," Romney was quick to respond. At a press conference, he said, "the characterization of Olympic matters as Mormon or non-Mormon is in my view both divisive and demeaning. . . . These are Games for America. . . . They're Episcopal. They're Catholic. They're Muslim. They're Jewish. They're Mormon. They're Baptist."[47] Second, determining the alcohol policy at the Olympic Games was tricky because "to attack another person's religion, in Utah that is done in an indirect manner talking about alcohol."[48] Although the LDS Church did not directly intervene, a compromise was reached between the Mormon and non-Mormon communities that permitted the limited use of alcohol during the Olympic Games.

The themes of Romney's experience as leader of the SLOC would reappear when he ran for president in 2008—the surprise at the rejection of his religious faith by non-Mormon Americans, the hostilities and suspicion between Mormon and non-Mormon communities, and the attacks on his religion via proxy issues like alcohol. But before he ran for president, Romney was elected governor of Massachusetts (2003–7), where he had to contend with

large Democratic majorities in both chambers of the state legislature.[49] Among his accomplishments as governor were balancing
the budget and reforming government agencies.[50] But these were
overshadowed by the passage of statewide health insurance legislation, which defined his tenure as governor. The health insurance
law was a market-based approach that extended coverage to all
citizens of Massachusetts: people were required to purchase health
insurance or face loss of their personal income tax exemption. It
also established means-tested state subsidies for people who either
lacked employer insurance or were below an income threshold. For
Romney, "we came up with a good solution to an intractable problem, and we did it without a government takeover and without a
massive tax increase. It was a big step forward, for Massachusetts
and for the nation."[51]

When Romney ran for the Republican presidential nomination
in 2008, he, like his father before him, was considered a frontrunner. Although he finished first among Republican voters in a
national poll, he would finish second in the Iowa caucuses to Mike
Huckabee in spite of outspending his rival by a margin of five-to-
one.[52] Romney would win the Wyoming and Maine caucuses and
the Nevada and Michigan primaries but then lose the New Hampshire and South Carolina primaries and, more importantly, Florida
to John McCain.[53] After his victory on Super Tuesday, February 5,
McCain cemented his status as the frontrunner. Romney ended his
campaign two days later and endorsed McCain.[54]

Romney lost the nomination primarily because he was unable
to present himself as an authentic conservative, as well as because
of unease among the Republican electorate about his religious faith.
In spite of endorsements from Rush Limbaugh and Ann Coulter,
Romney's changed positions on social issues like abortion, same-
sex marriage, and gun control made him vulnerable to the charge
of political opportunism made by his rivals John McCain and Mike
Huckabee.[55] Coinciding with his "flip-flopping" on issues important

to social conservatives was Romney's religious faith, which made some Americans uncomfortable and reinforced questions about his credentials as an authentic conservative.

In spite of repeated statements that he was loyal to the U.S. Constitution, Romney continued to face questions throughout the campaign as to whether his Mormon faith would interfere with his obligations as president.[56] No other political candidate at the time had to confront such questions. This difference in treatment between Mormon and non-Mormon politicians shows that the return of religion as an issue of political competence is also a return to religious intolerance. Although Mitt Romney, unlike Joseph Smith, did not have to worry about assassination because of his religious faith, he did have to confront religious prejudice from voters in the Republican Party.

As one would expect, Romney's political rivals took advantage of the public's suspicion about Mormonism. In December 2007, when asked whether the Mormon faith was a religion or a cult, Huckabee replied that he believed it was a religion despite his lack of knowledge about it, and then added, "Don't Mormons believe that Jesus and the devil are brothers?"[57] Later Huckabee issued a "non-apology apology"—an apology, according to political scientist Larry J. Sabato, in which "they're proving they're not sincere by continuing to raise the subjects. Once you apologize, you should avoid the subject like the plague. . . . It's no accident they [the Huckabee campaign] continue to bring these things up. . . . There is a strong prejudice among many fundamentalist Christians against Mormonism."[58] Other notable incidents where Romney's religious faith came up were the January 2008 Focus on the Family video, which stated that Romney "has acknowledged that Mormonism is not a Christian faith," and the Boca Raton debate, where Romney was confronted with the statistic that 44 percent of respondents in a poll stated that a Mormon would have a difficult time unifying the country.[59]

Romney addressed the subject directly on December 6, 2007, in a speech entitled "Faith in America" at the George Herbert Walker

Bush Presidential Library.[60] Modeled after John F. Kennedy's September 1960 pledge not to allow Catholic doctrine to inform U.S. policy, Romney's speech made the same pledge with reference to Mormonism. Although Romney declined to address the specifics of his religious faith except to say that the LDS "church's beliefs about Christ may not all be the same as those of other faiths," he did advocate a separation of church and state and declared that he would decline directives from churches, including the LDS Church, if elected president. Although the speech was widely praised by political commentators, it did little to help Romney in the Iowa caucus, where an estimated 40 percent of the Republican electorate identified themselves as evangelical Christians.[61]

In spite of his failure to secure the 2008 Republican presidential nomination, Mitt Romney appears to be poised for another attempt in 2012. He has kept much of his PAC money from the 2008 campaign, and he worked to elect Republican candidates in the 2010 midterm elections.[62] He won the 2012 presidential straw poll at the 2009 CPAC convention and the 2012 Southern Republican Leadership Conference straw poll in 2010.[63] His book *No Apology: The Case for American Greatness*, was released in March 2010, and he went on an eighteen-state book tour promoting. In this book, Romney outlines his blueprint for the United States in both domestic and foreign policy and solidifies his positions on issues that are important to social conservatives. He refers only infrequently to his religion, and then only in a bland, generic way that avoids some Americans' concerns about Mormonism.

Religious faith played a more pivotal role for Mitt Romney than it had for any other Mormon running for the presidency since the time of Joseph Smith. Like his father, Mitt Romney was an initial forerunner for his party's nomination; unlike his father, Mitt stayed in the race until it was decided.[64] In a time when religion has returned as a political issue and when social and religious voters constitute a significant portion of the Republican Party, Mitt Romney's Mormon faith had become a political liability. Whether

Romney will be able to define his political persona beyond his religion remains to be seen, especially if he runs for the nomination again in 2012.

Challenges from the Church and the Public

As national Mormon politicians have attempted to make their personas and positions more mainstream in order to be accepted in the United States, they have been accused by members of their own Church of having abandoned the true principles of their faith. For example, the political success of the Udall family—Morris (1922–1998), Stewart (1920–2010), Tom (b. 1948), and Mark (b. 1950)—has come at the cost of informally breaking with the Church. Self-described as "a one-eyed Mormon liberal from Arizona," Morris served fourteen terms in the U.S. House of Representatives. When he ran for the Democratic nomination for president in 1976 against Jimmy Carter,[65] he received bad press for his religion because of what were seen as racist tendencies within the LDS Church at the time.[66] Although the issue caused him to split informally with the Church, his Mormonism remained more than just a religion to him: it was a cultural heritage.[67] His brother, Stewart, was secretary of the interior under Presidents Kennedy and Johnson. He, too, was what he called a "Jack Mormon," or one who did not fully participate in the Church. Morris's son, Mark, and Stewart's son, Tom, are U.S. senators from Colorado and New Mexico, respectively. Both are formally affiliated with but personally disconnected from their Mormon faith. Mark Udall went so far as to turn his Mormonism into a cultural—not religious—appeal during his campaign. "Mormons were children of the West," he said, who focused on family, community, God, and the outdoors.[68] Tom also claims a link to the values of his Mormon upbringing, though he does not actively practice the religion. "I'm proud of my Mormon heritage," he said in a 2008 interview. "And my values and my value system . . . are very much a part of my approach to issues."[69] By transforming their Mormonism into a cultural legacy, the members of the Udall family have gained political acceptance in the United States, but at the cost of losing it as an active faith.

Besides the Udall and the Romney families, the most prominent Mormon politician in recent memory is Senator Harry Reid of Nevada, a Democrat who was first elected to the Senate in 1993 and currently serves as the Senate majority leader. Reid joined the LDS Church when he was in college and remains an active member today. Although some have criticized him for what they see as conflicting values between his political party and his faith, he actually sees the values as complementary.[70] "I think it is much easier to be a good member of the Church and a Democrat than a good member of the Church and a Republican," mostly because Democrats are better at helping others, he said in 2001.[71] Speaking about the influence that his Mormonism has had on his politics, Reid said, "I don't think you can separate your religion from your politics, it's part of your personality. It is part of who you are."[72] Determined to spread the word that being a good Democrat was not incompatible with being a good Mormon, Reid spoke to four thousand students at Brigham Young University in 2007. "My faith and political beliefs are deeply intertwined," he said. "I am a Democrat because I am a Mormon, not in spite of it."[73]

At first, Reid's voting record would suggest that his Mormon faith does not influence his politics; in 2008, Americans for Democratic Action rated him as 70 percent liberal, while the American Conservative Union rated him as 19 percent conservative.[74] But on specific issues, Reid often sides with the mainstream Mormon constituency. For example, Reid disagrees with *Roe v. Wade*. Speaking about his stance on the hot-button issue, he has said, "I clearly oppose abortion. . . . I think that my views are clear, and I think that I have worked very hard with groups all over America to reduce the number of unwanted pregnancies, and I'll continue to do that."[75]

Reid also sides with most Mormons on the issue of same-sex marriage and has voted in favor of the Defense of Marriage Act (although he voted against the proposed Federal Marriage

Amendment).[76] Above all else, Reid has said he values being true to his own beliefs: "The most important thing I can do as a leader is set an example with my own behavior." And unlike some of his fellow politicians, Reid has suffered from no sex scandals or accusations of public misconduct, despite a high level of scrutiny. His explanation for his clean-cut image is simple: "I pride myself on my integrity and always try to do what is right."[77]

Whereas the Udall family transformed their Mormonism into a cultural legacy in order to gain mainstream political acceptance, Reid has cherry-picked his issues, such as abortion and same-sex marriage, to remain true to his faith. As an active member, Reid consequently faces more challenges about his positions from within the Church. As Reid has shown, one can remain a devout Mormon and a Democrat, but the obstacles will come from within the LDS Church rather than from the American public.

Although the LDS Church does not officially endorse any political candidate or party, and does value helping the poor and caring for the land—values associated more with Democrats than with Republicans—its strong stance and active campaigning on social issues like abortion and same-sex marriage incline its members to be conservative and Republican.[78] Besides the Romneys, nationally the most famous Mormon Republican politicians are Orrin Hatch and Jon Huntsman. Because of their socially conservative values, Hatch and Huntsman have little to fear from members of their own religion but do face the challenge of a suspicious American public.

By his own account, Hatch should take the credit for reintroducing the possibility of a Mormon president.[79] As a sixth-term Republican senator from Utah, Hatch had garnered a great deal of experience from sitting on key committees, such as Judiciary, Intelligence, and Health Care, and his name had occasionally surfaced as a Supreme Court nominee. He entered the presidential race in 2000 with help from his Washington experience and conservative credentials. Unfortunately for him, Hatch was not widely known nationally and entered the race late, which caused his run for the presidency to be fairly short. Despite his poor showing, Hatch hoped that "his candidacy helped dispel some misconceptions about his religious faith."[80] In the press, Hatch was lauded as "a staunch conservative," known for his "high moral views."[81] Still, he felt misunderstood and disadvantaged. "There's real anti-Mormon prejudice out there," he said.[82] Throughout his campaign he worked to educate voters as to the true nature of his religion.[83] Despite his best efforts, Mormons did not come out in droves in support of Hatch, either. As he explained it, members of the LDS Church "are just not political, that's the problem. If I had to depend on my fellow Mormons, I would not have come this far."[84]

While Mormon politicians like Hatch, the Udalls, and the Romneys have struggled to overcome the bad press that came along with their faith, Jon Huntsman Jr. has been an exception. The eldest son of Utah billionaire and philanthropist Jon Huntsman Sr., Jon Jr. studied at the University of Utah and the University of Pennsylvania after dropping out of high school to be in a rock band. Huntsman's service to the LDS Church as a Mormon missionary in Taiwan taught him to speak Mandarin Chinese fluently and helped to prepare him for the ambassadorship to Singapore from 1992 to 1993. Later he brought his politics home to Utah, where he became governor in 2005. His November 2008 reelection was a rousing success, as he won 78 percent of the vote.[85]

Huntsman's popularity as governor is significant because his politics appear to be slightly to the left of the Mormon mainstream, although he considers himself a social conservative. His major accomplishment was a thorough reform of the state's health care. Using tax breaks and negotiation to keep prices reasonable, he managed private sector insurance firms and expanded health coverage to Utah's working poor. According to the *Washington Post*, the bipartisan project was "downright dreamy" and provided a workable model for national reform.[86] Huntsman also strayed from the Mormon majority—and the ideology of his own constituency—in his support of civil unions for same-sex couples,[87] which shocked Utahans at a time when the LDS Church was funding efforts in California to support Proposition 8, which would allow only marriages between a man and a woman to be recognized in the state. Clarifying what many thought to be a discrepancy in his moral positions, Huntsman said, "I'm a firm believer in the traditional construct of marriage, a man and a woman." For him, the greater issue was "enhancing equal rights for others in nontraditional relationships."[88]

Huntsman's middle-of-the-road, bipartisan popularity was not overlooked by President Barack Obama, who nominated Huntsman to serve as the U.S. ambassador to China in 2009.[89] In late 2009, a Chinese journalist asked him, "Who would get the credit if you do a good job as ambassador and go on to run for president in 2016? You or the man who selected you, President Barack Obama?" Huntsman replied with a smile, calling the question treacherous and unanswerable "because I don't do politics here."[90] However, after he had resigned his ambassdorship on April 30, 2011, Huntsman began his presidential bid for the 2012 Republican nomination. Although his campaign has fared poorly so far, Huntsman remains a potentially viable candidate and power for the next presidential cycle.

The challenges confronting national Mormon politicians depend upon which political party they belong to. For Democrats, with their more secular social values, Mormon politicians face obstacles within their own church. Some, like the Udalls, become inactive members and see their Mormonism as a cultural rather than religious legacy; others, like Reid, cherry-pick those issues, such as abortion and same-sex marriage, about which the Church seems to care most. For Republicans, given the strong association in the public's mind between the Republican Party and the LDS Church, the major opposition comes not from their church but from the American public. Mormon Republicans have to find a way to gain acceptance by the American public as Republicans first and Mormons second.

Are We Ready for a Mormon President?

Much has changed since Joseph Smith was the first Mormon to run for the presidency in 1844. More recent representatives of the Mormon faith, like the Udalls, the Romneys, Harry Reid, Orrin Hatch, and Jon Huntsman, have received mixed reviews from the American public. The question remains whether Americans are willing to vote for a Mormon for president. While cultural optimists may give credit to an ever-increasing tolerance and diversity among the voting public (as was evidenced in Barack Obama's historic win in 2008), the people themselves appear to be less generous. When asked in 2006, "Would you ever consider voting for a Mormon candidate in a presidential election?" 43 percent of Americans said no, 38 percent said yes, and 19 percent were not sure. The same poll also reported that 53 percent of evangelicals would not vote for a Mormon.[91] According to these polling data, bias against a Mormon candidate would virtually preclude him or her from winning a presidential election.

In 2008 Mitt Romney's presidential campaign struggled with the lingering effects of the unpopularity of his religion. In fact, some believe that if it were not for his religion and the prejudice against it, Romney might have been more successful. According to a writer for the *Canada Free Press*, Mitt Romney was "the most Republican, most conservative, most qualified, and most devoted person running." Furthermore, they described him as "decent, honest, and competent . . . the best candidate for the open position in the White House."[92] Similarly, a writer for the *Washington Monthly* saw Mitt as an ideal candidate, the kind Republicans dream of: "A social conservative from the most cerulean of blue states who can please the base while not scaring off the moderate."[93] Nevertheless, despite this early praise in the press and his unique combination of economic and political ability (made especially important in the recession that began in 2008), Romney was not able to overcome opposition against his religious beliefs. In an article titled

"No Mormons Need Apply," a writer for the *American Spectator* observed, "It now seems undeniable that religion played the key role in Mitt Romney's failure to win the Republican nomination, or, for that matter, to finish a close second."[94] A poll conducted by the *Los Angeles Times* and Bloomberg found that only Islam would be a more damaging faith for a prospective presidential candidate.[95]

But the reasons for lingering (and perhaps growing) political prejudice against members of the LDS Church are less clear. When asked if he believed a Mormon could be elected president, Alan Wolfe, director of Boston College's Boisi Center for Religion and American Public Life, granted that it was a "fascinating question" because Mormonism is "a quintessential American success story," although it is not popularly recognized as such.[96] Moreover, the religion has a deep attachment to America threaded throughout its doctrine. Former Church president Ezra Taft Benson (who served as secretary of agriculture under Dwight Eisenhower) called the Constitution "divinely inspired," a "sacred document," and a "heavenly banner."[97] This idea is founded in LDS scripture. In 1833 Smith received the word of the Lord, which said, "I have established the Constitution of this land by the hands of wise men whom I raised up unto this very purpose."[98] Members of the LDS Church believe that America is the modern-day "promised land" and that its people are blessed and protected by God. The freedoms granted by the American system of government are God-given, and upholding them is a sacred duty.[99]

In his book *A Mormon in the White House?* Hugh Hewitt lists what he believes are the greatest obstacles confronting Mormon politicians who possess presidential ambitions: (1) the idea that a Mormon president will take orders from Salt Lake City; (2) the idea that a Mormon president will promote the LDS Church's missionary work; (3) the strangeness of the religion itself.[100] In his "Faith in America" speech, Romney addressed the first two concerns, and he spoke to the third one in an interview with Hewitt, in which he recognized the fundamental theological differences between

Mormons and evangelicals but called for common enterprise on moral issues, such as abortion and same-sex marriage.[101] Romney and others also reject a religious test for those who seek political office. The hope is that as for Roman Catholics and Jews, the question of religion will recede in importance for Mormon political candidates.

4

AN AMERICAN THEOLOGY

Christianity and Culture

The contemporary importance of religion is evident in the abundance of religious organizations active in American politics and in attempting to define American culture. The political scientist Eldon J. Eisenach describes two cases where religion plays a role in both American politics and culture.[1] In the first case, religious groups operate like any other interest groups, such as labor unions, environmental groups, or the chamber of commerce, that seek recognition and advantage in social, cultural, and political struggle. In this sense, religious organizations are private groups that translate their beliefs, desires, and demands into public interest issues when they participate in social and political processes.

However, in the second case, religious organizations are unique in that they partake of the definition of a civilization's culture. They define the cultural basis of social and political processes so as to determine which values society should accept, which groups are included (or excluded) from mainstream society, and what defines social and political relations in America. From this perspective, religion is foundational to a social and political structure that is tolerant, pluralist, and democratic. American civilization cherishes the values of religious tolerance, social pluralism, separation of church and state because religious groups, among them many Christian groups, are instrumental in creating them.

Like most religious groups in the United States, the LDS Church can be understood from both perspectives. But what makes Mormons unique is that they have challenged and continue to challenge the cultural foundation of politics in the United States. With the exception of Muslim Americans, no other religious group asks whether the traditional understanding of the Judeo-Christian values that has influenced and shaped America's cultural foundation is correct. This disagreement stems from the unique theology of Mormonism, a theology that not only emerged in the United States but continues like no other to cause controversies among Christians and thereby raises broader political questions about tolerance and social pluralism in the United States.

This chapter will explore how Mormon theology and the Church's relationship to other religious groups both contribute to and question the cultural foundation of American civilization. Because of its recent origins and innovative teachings, Mormonism has had a contentious relationship with other religious groups in America, even though Mormon voters are aligned in their political beliefs and voting patterns with those at the conservative end of the spectrum.

A Recent History

A proper understanding of the place of Mormonism in American life must begin with a discussion of its history. Because the Mormon faith is less than two hundred years old, some elements of its foundational story are surrounded by controversy, and a number of questions exist about Joseph Smith, the Book of Mormon, and how the Mormon Christ differs from the Christ of mainline Protestantism.

Like many religious movements, the LDS Church had humble beginnings, though it began with extravagant claims. In the spring of 1820, a fourteen-year-old boy emerged from the woods in rural upstate New York with a story that would challenge the very foundations of religious belief in America. He was not a scholar and had no theological training. In fact, Joseph Smith had attended church meetings only a few times in his life, despite the overwhelming fervor of the "burned-over district" that surrounded him.[2] He attended camp meetings and Sunday services for various sects, but found himself dissatisfied by the way that the claims of each group seemed to contradict the others.[3]

Smith worried for his soul and felt compelled to be baptized into some church to ensure his eternal salvation. But still he was confused. He wondered, "What is to be done? Who of all these parties are right; or, are they all wrong together? If any one of them be right, which is it, and how shall I know it?"[4] One night, especially troubled by the tumult of religious sectarianism around him, Smith found special meaning in a passage he read in the New Testament: "'If any of you lack wisdom, let him ask of God. . . . .' Never did any passage of scripture come with more power to the heart of man than this did at this time to mine."[5]

Prompted by the promise of this verse, Smith decided to ask God which church he should join. Of the spectacular experience that followed, he later recounted:

> It was on the morning of a beautiful, clear day, early in the spring of eighteen hundred and twenty. It was the first time in my life that I had made such an attempt, for amidst all my anxieties I had never as yet made the attempt to pray vocally. After I had retired to the place where I had previously designed to go, having looked around me, and finding myself alone, I kneeled down and began to offer up the desires of my heart to God.[6]

In response to his simple question, Smith received an extraordinary answer: in a vision he saw God and Jesus Christ, who told him to join none of the churches because, as Christ told him, "they draw near to me with their lips, but their hearts are far from me."[7] They spoke to Smith as one man speaks to another, and called him by name. He described the beings as "personages," in the image of a man, "whose brightness and glory def[ied] all description."[8] This "first vision," as it came to be known, solidified many of what would later become among the key tenets of Smith's new religion; namely, that God was a being like a man, that the fullness of religious truth had been lost from the earth and needed to be restored, and that God speaks to man today.[9]

The revelation that none of the existent faiths pleased God was not much comfort to Smith. It would be up to him to usher in "the restoration of all things"—to bring back God's whole truth to the earth.[10] His vision was only the beginning of what would be a lifelong pursuit: to reestablish the truth that was missing from the earth. It was a passion he would suffer and eventually give his life for.[11] Throughout the remainder of his life, Smith was derided by local preachers and others to whom he confided the story of his revelation. But he kept up his work nonetheless, encouraged by his family and content to be an outsider if it meant doing what he believed to be right.[12]

Smith formally established his church on April 6, 1830, calling it the Church of Christ (later The Church of Jesus Christ of Latter-day Saints). Six Church members were present at that first meeting, which took place in the log cabin home of Peter Whitmer, a friend of Smith's. Shortly after that, missionaries were sent out to teach the gospel and spread the good news: that a prophet lives on the earth today, that God continues to speak to mankind, and that a new book of scripture (the Book of Mormon) had been discovered. As church membership grew, its problems steadily increased. Despite the fervor and enthusiasm of early converts, the Church's distinctive theology and condemnation of mainstream Christianity contributed to its continuing struggle for acceptance.

As a reaction to growing hostilities in New York, as well as in response to specific revelation given to Smith, Church members were encouraged to gather together to build Zion, a place ruled by the principles of the Mormon gospel where the spirit of God could dwell. In 1831, the group moved to Kirtland, Ohio, to join with a large group of converts in the area. Though they met with some success there, a number of revelations regarding the actual geographical location of Zion prompted Church members to move from Ohio to Missouri. However, the best efforts of the Mormon faithful to found Zion there were spoiled again as their unpopularity followed them west: though land was abundant on the frontiers, tolerance for Smith and his new religion was low, and violence often prompted the Church to give up its land and possessions and move on. In the end, due to persecutions and hostilities, including an extermination order against Mormons issued by Illinois governor Lilburn Boggs, Zion would not be built in New York, Ohio, Missouri, or Illinois.[13] Each time the congregation was ousted by its neighbors, it fled farther west, toward the edges of "civilization" and the borders of the American wilderness. However, even among the rugged frontiersmen, the Mormons could not find any acceptance. Violence often broke out between the Mormons and their neighbors over issues such as the practice of polygamy or Smith's theocratic-political leadership.[14] Smith himself was tarred and feathered, families were terrorized, crops were ruined, printing presses were destroyed, and an entire community was massacred at Haun's Mill. Eventually, Smith himself was killed at the hands of an angry mob of his neighbors.

Mormon Theology

The violence and prejudice Smith and others suffered was largely ascribable to reactions to what others saw as a peculiar Mormon

theology that claimed to be Christian, yet differed from mainstream Protestantism and Catholicism in significant ways. Most
notable, perhaps, were the addition of "new" Mormon scripture
(the Book of Mormon), the Mormon idea of Christ, and corre-
sponding views on the afterlife and the eternal nature of mankind.
However, Mormons would argue that these differences are not as
alienating as they seem and that their beliefs are complementary to,
and represent a fulfillment of, the Abrahamic tradition.

The Book of Mormon is perhaps the most obvious theological
departure by Mormonism from mainstream Christianity. According to Smith and his followers, this new book of scripture, "another
testament of Jesus Christ" to complement the Old and New Testaments of the Bible,[15] is a translation of ancient records given to
Smith in 1827. The records themselves are a compilation of over a
thousand years of history edited by the fourth-century American
prophet Mormon (thus giving the book its name). It was published
in 1830 with the help of Smith family friend Martin Harris, who
mortgaged his farm in order to fund the project.[16] According to
Mormon belief, the book contains the fullness of the gospel of Jesus
Christ. Its themes are similar to those found in the Old and New
Testaments, but the LDS Church asserts that the Book of Mormon
is "the most correct of any book," one that will bring men nearer to
God than any other book if they abided by its precepts.[17]

The Book of Mormon tells the story of an ancient people,
descended from the Israelites, who were warned by God to flee
Jerusalem six hundred years before the birth of Christ. They traveled to a new promised land in the Americas, where they lived
and thrived socially, culturally, and economically for nearly one
thousand years.[18] It contains information regarding the spiritual
and physical welfare of this people, who had prophets among them
who taught both the old law of Moses and the new law of Jesus
Christ even before his mortal ministry. The dramatic climax of
the book comes when Christ appears to the people after his life in
Jerusalem and his death and resurrection. He teaches the gathered

crowds many of the same lessons that are familiar to scholars of the New Testament (the Sermon on the Mount, for example, is largely repeated here), and allows them to feel of the nail prints in his hands and feet and the wound in his side—testaments to the maltreatment he had received in the Old World and the suffering he had borne for the salvation of mankind.

The distinctive LDS perception of Christ is central to the debates regarding the Church's position as a Christian denomination. Importantly, the Mormon Church message focuses on Jesus Christ, whom they believe to be the creator of the world and the personal savior of mankind. He is a separate entity from God the Father, who is also interested and involved in the affairs of his sons and daughters on this earth. Both speak to mankind today as they did in times of old and, along with the Holy Ghost (the third member of the Godhead), are eternal beings and unchangeable. Interestingly, the LDS stories of Christ do not begin, as do many histories of Jesus, with his virgin birth, nor do they end with his ascension into heaven after his resurrection. Instead, they encompass the entire LDS vision of Christ, from his premortal role and ministry to his modern manifestations and revelations to Mormon prophets.[19] This is the LDS Christ—not limited to or even fully defined by his mortal life. His is life everlasting, and no history can contain the fullness of his works. This theology of Christ encourages unique LDS interpretations of the joint significance of spirit, body, and mortality.

LDS stories of Christ usually begin in the premortal existence, where all who are now on earth lived before they came here. All were spirit children of God, but they were not made by him. Here again is another key LDS departure from mainstream Christian creeds: the LDS God is not a creator.[20] He organized existing matter to form the earth (thus giving matter itself a spirituality, as it is coeternal with God), and likewise organized the spirits of men, who, through this act, became his children.[21] As Harold Bloom explains it, this theology is deeply rooted in the American experience: "The God of the American religion [Mormonism] is not a creator-God, because the American never *was* created, and so the American has at least part of the God within herself."[22]

Additionally, LDS theology supports the idea that each individual has the potential to become like God. Just months before his death, Smith proclaimed this controversial theory at the funeral of a friend. Though reinterpreted and expanded upon in the decades that followed, it is perhaps still one of the least understood of LDS theologies, even among Church members.[23] The LDS argue that this particular theology of man's god-like potential does not in any way demote God, nor does it necessarily promote man to God's status. Instead, they understand that men can become "as God," not become God himself—specifically, that their potential is to become "gods" with a lower-case "g."[24]

Interestingly, the potential for all men to become gods (if they are righteous) does not diminish the role of Christ in the LDS Church. The LDS story of Christ begins in the premortal existence, when God told the spirits that they needed to come to earth to procure a body (the body being essential for eventual exaltation and godliness). He knew that sending the spirits to earth would cause some of them to rebel, so he planned to provide a savior for them. Jesus himself (as a premortal spirit) advocated for the plan and chose to be God's sacrifice for the immortality of all his children. Thus, Jesus Christ was a leader from before his birth.

Neither did his mission or ministry end with his mortal life. According to LDS theology (as evidenced in the Book of Mormon), Christ appeared to people in the New World shortly after his resurrection, bringing them the same teachings he shared with the Jews in Jerusalem during his lifetime. More recently, the LDS Christ appeared to Joseph Smith and gave him instruction. Other Latter-day Saint prophets and leaders have testified of Christ, and some claim to have seen him in visions.[25] The LDS Christ continues to busy himself actively working for the salvation of mankind: he is not finished with the world.

Despite these and other differences, LDS depictions of Christ are much like those of other Christians. For example, they believe in his virgin birth and follow the precepts of his mortal ministry in Jerusalem as described in the New Testament. The LDS vision of Christ is constantly working for the salvation of his people, saving their souls and paying the price for their sins through his atoning sacrifice, though his work is not yet done. In fact, his work will not be finished in any time foreseeable to man. To further his work, he speaks to man today and sits as the figurative head of the LDS Church.

The LDS perspectives of God as organizer and of Christ's work as eternal are both reflected in related doctrines and practices. For them, the Christ who actively works to save the souls of men inspires his followers on earth to do the same, whether that work is building cities, raising families, or preaching the gospel at home or abroad. Because their understanding of Christ reaches both before and after his mortal ministry, LDS members see themselves as eternal beings also. This "eternal perspective," as many call it, colors their worldview and either amplifies or denigrates the experiences of this world. It inspires their action, for they believe that their potential is to one day be as God is, if they live worthy lives.

Members of the LDS Church believe that life continues after death in a manner that is slightly different from mainstream Christian beliefs. After a person dies, his or her spirit resides in either a prison or paradise, where it awaits final judgment. At this point, the individual will be resurrected, meaning that the spirit will be reunited with the body. Where this newly resurrected body ultimately resides is dependent on the faithfulness of each individual. There is no real "hell" to speak of in LDS theology, only "outer darkness," which is characterized as being cut off from the light and presence of God, Christ, and the Holy Ghost. The LDS concept of heaven is made up of three separate degrees of glory, each more wonderful than the last. In the highest kingdom, known as Celestial, a person may dwell with God the Father and Jesus Christ.

Here, family relationships continue beyond the grave. Husbands, wives, brothers, and sisters will be reunited to live together forever.

This emphasis on family bonds that continue beyond the grave underscores the importance of familial relations in the LDS Church and is reflected in LDS temple worship, where couples are married for time and all eternity (rather than "until death do us part"). Temples are different from regular meetinghouses in a number of ways. A meetinghouse may be a specially dedicated building or a rented space that hosts local congregations for Sunday services and weekly meetings, including social activities. Any person, whether Mormon or not, may enter an LDS meetinghouse. By contrast, temples are reserved for faithful members of the Church who have demonstrated their worthiness through a series of personal interviews with local priesthood authorities. No regular worship services are offered in the temple; in fact, LDS temples are closed on Sundays so that Church members may attend their regular meetings and spend time with family. The function of temples is to do "work," meaning to conduct saving ordinances for the living and the dead. For example, Church members believe that every person must be baptized in order to obtain salvation. In temples, they may act as proxies for their dead ancestors and be baptized on their behalf.[26]

Baptism in the LDS Church—whether for the living or the dead—is only recognized if done by the proper authority. This authority is the priesthood, which Joseph Smith taught was lost sometime after the death of Christ's apostles. It was restored in latter days by Peter, James, and John, who appeared to Smith and laid hands on his head to bestow the gift of the priesthood on him. Today, the priesthood is a privilege reserved for worthy men over the age of twelve that allows for them to officiate in sacred ordinances and serve in leadership positions. Women do not hold or exercise priesthood authority and so hold limited positions of power in Church governance.

Though there are many more important differences between LDS theology and that of mainstream Christianity, the seeds of each of them may be found in the key principles discussed above. The rejection of other religions (even Protestant), the discovery of "new" scripture, the particular understanding of the role of Christ, and the potential of mankind (including the possibility of eternal family relationships) all point to a significant departure from popular Christian systems of belief. However, the LDS argue that despite these distinctions, they are in fact a Christian religion because they believe that Christ is the son of God, sent to save the world, and that he stands at the head of the Church today.

Common Politics, Religious Prejudice

Because of these theological differences, Mormonism's relationship with mainstream Christianity has evolved into a reluctant and schizophrenic tolerance. On the one hand, the LDS Church's positions on certain social and political issues, like abortion and same-sex marriage, are similar to those of other conservative Christian denominations and make it a potent ally in waging the cultural wars. On the other hand, the LDS Church's beliefs, and the source of those beliefs, run contrary to the theology of mainstream Christianity and cause it to be viewed with suspicion. Mormon scripture, the belief in ongoing revelation, and a henotheistic conception of God alienate Mormons from mainstream Christians and are the source of conflict between them.

The practical alliance between Mormons and conservative Christians is best illustrated by the voting patterns of religious voters in past presidential elections. According to the Pew Research Forum, over 60 percent of Mormons have voted for the Republican candidate for president in the last two election cycles, which places them in the same company as white evangelical Protestant voters (whether weekly observant or less observant) and weekly attending mainline Protestants and Catholics.[27] By contrast, secular and unaffiliated believing voters, black Protestants, less observant white and Hispanic Catholics, and Jews tend to vote for the Democratic candidate for president.

On social issues, Mormons are actually more conservative than mainstream Christians. Eighty-eight percent of Mormons believe there are absolute standards of right and wrong (compared to 77 percent of the general population), and 68 percent of Mormons believe their values are being threatened by Hollywood, with only 54 percent of Jehovah's Witnesses and 53 percent of evangelical Protestants agreeing (compared to 42 percent of the general population).[28] Seventy percent of Mormons are opposed to abortion (compared to 42 percent of the general population); 68 percent say homosexuality should be discouraged rather than accepted by society, which is higher than evangelical Protestants (64 percent) and Muslims (61 percent); and 75 percent disagree that evolution is the best explanation of human life (only Jehovah's Witnesses are higher, at 90 percent).[29]

Sixty percent of Mormons claim to be conservative, and only 10 percent identify themselves as liberal (compared to 37 percent and 10 percent of the general population respectively); and 65 percent of Mormons identify themselves or lean towards the Republican Party, which is 15 percent higher than evangelical Protestants and 30 percent higher than the general population.[30] These conservative and Republican tendencies translate into political positions on the size and role of government and other issues. For example, 56 percent of Mormons prefer smaller government (compared to 43 percent of the general population), 49 percent of Mormons believe the government should do more for the needy (compared to 62 percent of the general population), and 54 percent of Mormons think the government should do more to protect morality (compared to 40 percent of the general population).

It is only on environmental issues and church involvement in politics that Mormons are aligned with the general population. Fifty-five percent of Mormons believe that environmental laws are worth the cost (compared to 61 percent of the general population).[31] Forty-eight percent of Mormons say that churches should stay out of politics (compared to 46 percent of the general population), while 47 percent believe that religious bodies should be able to express their views daily on social and political questions (compared to 50 percent of the general population). It should come as no surprise that Mormons share similar views with the general population on these two issues. Suffering from religious persecution for most of their history, Mormons can be ambivalent about church involvement into politics because it may draw more attention to their religion.

Interestingly, converts to Mormonism are less likely than lifelong members to identify themselves as either Republicans or conservative. Only 52 percent of converts identified themselves as Republicans, and 59 percent of them opposed abortion, compared to 69 percent and 74 percent, respectively, of lifelong members.[32] There also are some generational differences: 74 percent of Mormons under 50 oppose abortion, compared to 62 percent of Mormons over 50. However, younger Mormons are less likely to favor smaller government than older Mormons (50 percent to 67 percent) and less likely to describe themselves as ideologically conservative (57 percent to 66 percent).

Being more conservative and more Republican than any other religious voters makes Mormons a natural ally of conservative Christians on certain social and political issues. However, when it comes to actually voting for a Mormon political candidate, especially for president, Mormons faced overwhelming prejudice. Twenty-five percent of people polled expressed reservations when asked whether they would vote for a Mormon candidate for president, a number higher than for any group except atheists (61 percent) and Muslims (45 percent).[33] By comparison, 16 percent expressed reservations about voting for an evangelical, 11 percent for a Jew, and 7 percent for a Catholic. Furthermore, evangelicals, who value religiosity in a president the most, are the least likely to vote for a Mormon candidate (36 percent). When Mitt Romney ran for the 2008 presidential nomination for the Republican Party, his favorability ratings among those who had no reservations about voting for a Mormon dropped from 84 to 54 percent after questions began to emerge about his Mormon faith.

This result should be expected, since only Muslims (46 percent) and atheists (35 percent) are viewed less favorably than Mormons (53 percent) as viable presidential candidates.[34] By contrast, 60 percent of people have a favorable view of evangelicals, and 76 percent have a favorable view of Catholics and Jews. Although there are no partisan differences in the overview of Mormons (the favorable view of Mormons by Republicans, Democrats, and independents ranges from 53 percent to 55 percent), there are significance differences among religious groups. White mainline Protestants (62 percent) and white non-Hispanic Catholics (59 percent) expressed favorable views of Mormons, but only 46 percent of white evangelical Protestants have favorable views, and 39 percent unfavorable.

The explanation for these views is that only 52 percent of the public says that Mormonism is a Christian religion, while 31 percent claim it is not.[35] Forty-five percent of white evangelical Protestants believe Mormonism is not a Christian religion, while 40 percent believe it is. The number goes up to 52 percent of white evangelical Protestants who attend service at least once a week. By contrast, white mainline Protestants (62 percent) and white non-Hispanic Catholics (59 percent) see Mormonism as a Christian religion. Those with no religious affiliation also say Mormonism is a Christian religion (59 percent). However, even those who claim Mormonism is a Christian religion tend to see it as very different from their own religion (62 percent), while only a few say their religions share much in common (25 percent). This difference is especially pronounced among white evangelical Protestants, 67 percent of whom reject the idea that their religion shares much in common with Mormonism (compared to 61 percent of white non-Hispanic Catholics and 56 percent of white mainline Protestants).

Differences beyond Polygamy

When people were asked to describe Mormonism in a single word, words with negative associations outscored positive ones 27 percent to 23 percent, with 19 percent being neutral. The most commonly associated negative word for Mormons was "polygamy" or some reference to plural marriage (75 percent).[36] "Cult" was the next most commonly associated negative word (57 percent). Conversely, "family" or "family values" was the most commonly associated positive word for Mormons (74 percent), with "dedicated" (34 percent), "devote" (32 percent), and "faith" (25 percent) as runners-up. These associations should be expected given that only 49 percent of the public know a great deal about Mormonism. Simply put, what little the American public does know about Mormonism, it has reservations about.

But for those who have studied Mormonism, there are significance differences about the source and nature of divine authority, differences that lead to theological disagreement and raise questions regarding what constitutes Christianity. Perhaps the group that has most engaged Mormonism in theological debates and discussions is white evangelical Protestants,[37] who have criticized Mormons for relying upon extra-biblical traditions, such as the Book of Mormon, and therefore "following the late medieval Catholic pattern of favoring tradition over scripture."[38] By rejecting the *sola scriptura* principle, Mormons have mixed the words of man (Joseph Smith and other modern prophets) with the words of God. However, evangelical Protestants also have used tradition in the interpretation of the Bible and theological tenets, like the Apostle's Creed.[39] Likewise, Mormons, who criticize evangelicals for using early creeds to assist them in the interpretation of the Bible, have their own creeds.[40] Bruce McConkie, a Mormon elder and apologist, has stated that Joseph Smith's Fifth Lecture on Faith (winter 1834–35) "in effect, is a creed announcing who Deity is."[41] It is also hard not to conclude that "The Articles of

Faith of the Church of Jesus Christ of Latter-day Saints" is a creed. Its thirteen statements, like most creeds, list the most important beliefs of the Church.[42]

The question, therefore, that lies at the heart of the disagreement between Mormons and evangelical Protestants (and, more broadly, mainline Christians) is which tradition to accept as the legitimate source of divine authority: the one based on the traditional Christian Bible or the one that includes Mormon scripture and divine revelation. As Stephen Robinson, a Mormon scholar, has said, "What separates Latter-day Saints from Evangelicals is less our view of the nature of scripture and more our view of the canon."[43] Jan Shipps, a non-Mormon scholar, agrees and has argued that Mormonism is a departure from existing Christian tradition as much as early Christianity was a departure from Judaism, because Mormonism abandoned both Catholic and Protestant beliefs about the finality of the New Testament.[44] Philip Barlow also concurs with Shipps' assessment that Mormonism's departure from *sola scriptura* creates a new tradition that places limits on traditional biblical authority by rejecting it as a sufficient religious guide.[45]

What is interesting is that LDS members often do not see the question of tradition or canonicity as the distinguishing feature of their religion; rather, they cite the process of ongoing revelation. For example, Terryl Givens proposes that Mormonism alone, among those groups claiming to be Christian, is the only one that "still believe[s] in ongoing revelation."[46] And LDS leader Dallin Oaks states, "For us, the scriptures are not the ultimate source of knowledge, but what precedes the ultimate source. The ultimate knowledge comes by revelation . . . through those we sustain as prophets, seers, and revelators."[47] But the question of continuous revelation needs to be clarified, for other Christian religions also claim ongoing revelation. As the Mormon scholar Robert Millet points out,

Roman Catholics believe God continues to reveal his will and way through popes, councils, and the Catholic tradition as it develops by the work of the Holy Spirit. Pentecostals and charismatics believe that the gift of prophecy is still being poured on believers all over the world, and particularly in their meetings. Evangelicals of all sorts believe in the "illumination" of the Spirit, whereby the third person of the Trinity gives fresh and sometimes new understanding of the Written Word.[48]

The question, therefore, is not between closed versus ongoing revelation but the nature of revelation itself. For the LDS Church, revelation to a particular person in the nineteenth century, Joseph Smith, is similar to the forms of revelation that other Christian religions claim. What is perhaps more controversial is the LDS Church's claim that these new revelations supplant the widespread agreement among Christians regarding what constitutes the source, nature, and teaching of its religion.

The LDS Church's justification for interpreting the Bible through the lens of Mormon scripture is the primacy given to revelation for authority and the fallibility of recorded language. Stephen Robinson writes, "The direct revelation to a prophet or an apostle is immediate and primary. . . . However, the recording, transmission and interpretation of the word depends on fallible human beings, using the fallible tools of reason and language. . . . The [LDS] church's guarantee of doctrinal correctness lies primarily in the living prophet, and only secondarily in the preservation of the written text."[49] What is required is a new authority to interpret the biblical text that had been misunderstood until the nineteenth century. The LDS Church is not simply affirming the earlier teaching of Christianity; rather, it supplants it with new ones, as Robinson attests: "The Joseph Smith translation (JST) [of the traditional Bible] should be understood to contain additional revelation, alternate readings, prophetic commentary, or midrash, harmonization, clarification, and corrections . . . to the originals."[50] Indeed, this has been the Mormon claim from its inception: that the "plain and precious truths" were removed from the Bible before its final compilation (1 Nephi 13:26, Moses 1:40-41).

Mainstream Christians ask how this could be the case when there is no historical evidence of Mormon texts being excluded from the Bible, even as new and apocryphal documents from that time period have emerged.[51] Gerald R. McDermott presents the argument that mainstream Christians often use when disputing that Mormonism is a Christian religion.[52] The Jesus of Palestine has at least four gospels that testify to his existence and were written in the same century by people with a close connection to him. By contrast, the Jesus of the LDS Church has only a single document to attest to his existence and was written by someone eighteen centuries later who had no connection to him.[53] Furthermore, there are inconsistencies between the texts that attest to Jesus' existence and inconsistencies in the messages between the Palestinian Jesus and the LDS Jesus. For example, the LDS Jesus designates America as the new Israel and as the new Jerusalem and conceives of God as three separate deities rather than as a triune being. In short, according to the critics of Mormonism, because Mormon beliefs diverge widely from mainstream Christianity, and the principal source for its claim of authority, Mormon scripture, lacks credibility, Mormonism cannot be considered a Christian religion.

Some mainstream Christians have even compared Mormonism to Islam as a new type of religion.[54] Whereas Islam, with its new set of revelations that were written down in the Qur'an, derives from both Judaism and Christianity, Mormonism likewise received a new set of revelations that corrected both Jewish and Christian scriptures. Like Muslims, Mormons claim to be the true descendents of Abraham and claim a God that is nontriune in nature. Although polygamy is no longer practiced by mainstream Mormons, it still is by Muslims who live in countries where it is legal. Perhaps because of these similarities, the relations between the two religious groups can be characterized as friendly, with Muslims trying to learn from the LDS Church how to be accepted more by mainstream American society.[55]

Unlike the Muslims, who accept the LDS as part of the Abrahamic tradition, Jews do not.[56] Rejecting the claim that Mormons are members of the House of Israel, Jews believe that the tribal affiliation has been lost to antiquity (except in the case of the Levites and Cohens). They do not accept the Mormon belief in the Tribe of Mannasseh who migrated to America, or the Mormon claim that many members are of the Tribe of Ephraim.[57] In spite of these theological differences, both the LDS Church and Jewish groups desire peaceful coexistence, with the latter finding conversion inappropriate and offensive.

The most publicized controversy between Jews and Mormons has centered over the LDS Church's practice of baptizing the dead. Under Mormon theology, vicarious performance of baptism allows one's ancestors the option to accept or reject the saving ordinances of Mormon beliefs to achieve exaltation. Although it is contrary to LDS Church policy, there have been occasionally zealous LDS genealogists who have submitted the names of prominent individuals, including the Holocaust's Jewish victims. When this information became publicly known, Jewish groups found the practice offensive to their beliefs, as attempting to contact the dead is forbidden under Jewish law. As a result of public pressure, the LDS Church in 1995 established new policies that would stop the practice unless it was specifically requested or approved by relatives of victims.[58] However, the controversy still continues, as questions linger as to whether certain Jewish names have been removed from the LDS International Genealogical Index.[59] A joint Jewish-Mormon committee was formed to resolve this issue, but it has only generated animosity on both sides, and the issue has not been satisfactorily resolved.[60]

* * *

The question whether Mormonism is a Christian denomination or a non-Christian religion, like Judaism and Islam, remains a subject of dispute among many Americans. Which side one takes depends on one's views of the nature and authority of revelation and conception of divinity. Whereas mainstream Christians subscribe to the Bible and a triune God, Mormons accept extrabiblical sources as authoritative and a nontriune conception of God. There are also other theological differences between traditional Christians and Mormons, such as whether the universe was created *ex nihilo* (out of nothing), the meaning of the Garden of Eden, and the relationship between human beings and their own divinity. Certainly this book will not resolve these questions. However, it is worthwhile to clarify the theological differences among these religious groups in the hope they can understand, respect, and even learn from their unique traditions.

In practical terms, these theological differences have little impact on the voting patterns or positions on social and political issues that Mormons and other conservative religious groups share. Both groups are opposed to abortion and same-sex marriage and favor smaller government except in the protection of certain cultural values. The one exception to this political alliance is the question of whether conservative Christians, particularly white evangelical Protestants, will vote for a Mormon candidate for the presidency. Thus far the data do not suggest they would. Yet it is still undetermined whether religious belief or political calculation will triumph among these voters.

The American public's acceptance of Mormons' role in politics and its reservations about Mormon religious beliefs raise questions about the limits of religious tolerance in a democracy. One can recall that the American public had similar reservations about Catholics before John F. Kennedy was elected to the presidency in 1960 or about Jewish candidates before Joe Lieberman was nominated as the Democratic Party's vice-presidential candidate in 2000. It remains to be seen whether the same tolerance will be extended to Mormons after one is nominated as a presidential candidate by a major political party in this country.

By asking what constitutes the essence of Christianity—its source of revelation, the role of Christ, and the potentiality of human beings—Mormons have indirectly asked whether the cultural foundation of American civilization is correct. This challenge has not gone unnoticed; Mormons face prejudice even as they continue their attempt to be assimilated fully into American civilization. Over time, this prejudice has evolved into acceptance with reservations. Currently, Mormons are regarded with a balance of accommodation and suspicion, with pragmatic alliances formed between them and other Americans on certain social and political issues against a background of unease. Whether this will change will depend upon whether Americans accept Mormonism as a Christian—and therefore American—religion.

5

MORMONISM AS THE AMERICAN NARRATIVE

An American Story

When Alexis de Tocqueville arrived in America in 1831, he was immediately struck by its intense "religious atmosphere."[1] He had the luck to arrive in New York City at the height of the religious activity known as the Second Great Awakening, and he observed the democratic nature of American religion from one extreme to another as he traveled across the nation: from raucous holy rollers to pious priests and everything in between. Given the generous standard for what was considered not only politically but also socially acceptable, he reasoned of religious practice in the United States that "if it does not give [Americans] the taste for freedom, it singularly facilitates their use of it."[2] It was his perception that American religion was central to the function and ideology of democracy, both the way it is theorized and the way that theory is translated into practice in stabilizing American institutions like the government. He found that religion operated differently in

America, primarily because "the spirit of religion and the spirit of freedom" were not in conflict here. Instead, they were "united intimately with one another: they reigned together on the same soil."[3] In fact, Tocqueville reasoned that the "democratic and republican" habits of religion in America combined with a sense of piety to make the United States "the place in the world where the Christian religion has most preserved genuine power over souls."[4]

At the time of Tocqueville's visit, the Mormon religion was just one year old. Membership was small, and those who practiced Mormonism were a notable exception to the general feeling of religious pluralism that Tocqueville experienced. Yet the religion itself—its doctrines, structures, culture, and social practices— had much in common with the more mainstream values of the era in which it was founded. In this sense, the story of Mormonism is, in many respects, a story of America itself. In recent years, scholars have called it "a very American gospel," "intensely patriotic," "a religious version of the American Dream,"[5] "a theology of Americanism,"[6] "quintessentially American,"[7] and "the American religion":[8] all because it is so firmly rooted in the spirit and ideology of Jacksonian America.[9] According to Harold Bloom, "what matters most about Joseph Smith is how American both the man and his religion have proved to be," not only because they were intensely patriotic, but also because they and America as a whole relied on similar foundations of faith, industry, and individualism.[10] Some even argue that the Mormon faith is more American than other more commonly practiced faiths in the United States, and that its particular combination of spiritualism and patriotism makes Mormons "American nationalists of a peculiar sort."[11] Others have said that Mormonism was "the first American religion" because the religion "was brand new, with a new identity," like America itself.[12]

There are other specific ways in which the story of Mormonism and the story of America are similar. Most significantly, the tragedy and triumph of the LDS Church are much like what the nation as a whole was experiencing at the same historical moment. The Age of Jackson, during which Smith's religion made its debut, was a period of radical change.[13] Thanks in part to the Second Great Awakening, religious revivalism was a strong political and social force in many parts of the country. Additionally, the freedoms of new land and a new country inspired many to try their hands at their own cultural experiments—some religious, others secular, many communal.[14] Taken together, the politics and spirit of the age set the stage for great expectations and high hopes. During this period, the independently minded American had the audacity to dream of wealth and comfort as the by-products of his or her own industry and determination.[15] Many were successful in such ventures. Others were not. For decades, the Mormons followed their dreams to become the people they wanted to be, and, as for many other societies founded during the same period, what victories they won are wholly ascribable to their own hard work.

Joseph Smith, founder of the LDS Church, is an excellent example of the Jacksonian hero. Born in obscurity to a poor family in rural New England, Smith spent his days working the land with his father and brothers. He had almost no formal schooling, and little prospect of making any lasting imprint on the society in which he lived. And yet, more than one hundred and fifty years after his death, millions around the world revere him as a prophet. Like Jackson himself, Smith worked hard, embodied the industry and determination of his generation, and dreamed big. He pulled himself up by his bootstraps and labored to make his mark on the world around him. Despite difficulty, he ultimately believed in freedom and democracy and his own inherent right to build the society he envisioned. He shrugged off naysayers and continued to work. Such a rags-to-riches success story is part of the American dream.

From Smith onward, much of Mormon culture was assimilated from nineteenth-century U.S. culture, so much so that it reflects American ideologies in its doctrine and reenacts them in its own history. Mormons lived on the frontier and conquered their own corner of the Wild West, thereby fulfilling another portion of the American dream. Like generations of Americans before them, they wandered far from home and sacrificed greatly for the freedom to live and worship as they saw fit. They had (and continue to have) a reverential respect for the U.S. system of government, a patriotism born in the very fiber of their doctrines.

Additionally, they firmly believed in and practiced a form of manifest destiny, akin to the same spirit that contributed to the expansion of the United States westward to the Pacific Ocean during the same period.[16] Much like its mother country, the Mormon religion wanted space and the freedom to spread its message and image by expanding its borders. While most of the nation was caught up in the idea of forging new frontiers and populating the entire continent, none practiced these beliefs more faithfully than the Mormons. According to one historian, the Mormon religion "was infused with a great deal of spread-eagle American nationalism at a time when Manifest Destiny had become the watchword of the nation."[17] This is apparent in the westward movement of the Church, eventually into what was at the time Mexican territory, and its significant role in settling land west of the Rocky Mountains. This movement and industry were guided by a desire among the Mormons for a land of their own, and largely motivated by their pursuit of the freedom to rule themselves at a safe distance from those who would "hurt or make afraid."[18]

Furthermore, early Church members saw themselves as part of the divine destiny of the United States, and they took the ideology of expansion personally, implementing it in their communities and even in their own homes. For example, non-Mormons in early America generally had much larger families than their counterparts in England and Europe. Tocqueville noted that this might be because so much land needed to be filled, with no scarcity of resources or potential inheritance present to check growth. It was not unusual for American families of the period to have six, seven, or more children—even with a high rate of infant mortality on the frontier.[19] But the Mormons outdid themselves when they adopted wholeheartedly this American ideal. Perhaps because they were intent on populating their own cities and territories, Mormons had extremely large families, even compared to their contemporaries. Of course, much of this population boom was facilitated by the practice of polygamy (a practice officially ended in 1890), which allowed one man to father as many as thirty or more children (sometimes sixty or more).[20] Mormon cultural practices and theological doctrines such as these reflected and supported a nineteenth-century American perspective on the world. According to one commentator, the LDS Church, by "encapsulating these themes in revelation . . . sacralized and legitimated the utopian nationalism of nineteenth century Americans."[21] Such correlations between Jacksonian-era American values and past and present Mormon theology and practice reveal an underlying spirit of hope, optimism, and faith in the individual that helped to shape the Mormon faith and the American people as a whole.

An American Faith

Smith himself believed that the fates of the land and his religion were intertwined and that both had a divine purpose.[22] In fact, he "saw his new religion as a total response to all aspects, spiritual and material, of frontier life."[23] In many ways, Mormon theology reveres America in a way no other religion does. First, according to LDS doctrine, America was the original home of Adam, Eve, and the Garden of Eden.[24] Later, it became a promised land for God's chosen people—a branch of Israel warned by God to leave Jerusalem around 600 B.C., before its destruction.[25]

The Americas were a chosen promised land that offered religious freedom and great blessings for the people for as long as they were faithful. However, as the Book of Mormon forewarns, once the people have forgotten God, they will be removed from the land. Current members of the LDS Church take this as a personal warning to themselves as well as a more general admonition regarding the Lord's expectations for the United States.

The chosenness of America in LDS theology continues into modern times. For instance, Mormons believe that the founders of this nation were inspired to create a government based on principles of freedom and agency. The Constitution is a "heavenly banner" and a divinely inspired document that created a social, religious, and political environment that allowed Smith to bring forth the gospel.[26] During the early years of the Church, members sought to establish Zion in various locations as they traveled west, ultimately choosing the Salt Lake Valley as their own portion of the Promised Land and the modern-day headquarters of the Church. Mormons also believe that at the end of time, Christ will return to earth to rule his people from the New Jerusalem, which will be built in what is now known as Jackson County, Missouri.

All of this focus on the American continents makes Mormonism a peculiarly nationalist religion. Far from being disinterested in the political affairs of its home country, the LDS Church focuses intently on its founding principles and future prospects. But this does not mean that it lacks interest in the world outside of the nation's borders. Because the sect was new and small at first, it relied heavily on proselytizing and missionary work. From the very beginning of Mormonism, soon after the Book of Mormon was published, Smith sent members out into the world as missionaries. At first they stayed nearby, making converts in Pennsylvania and the rest of New England.[27] Within a few years, they were sent to Canada and England, eventually bringing thousands of converts back to the United States.[28] By stretching the borders of the Church's membership, the Mormons believed that they were metaphorically enlarging the stakes of Zion and heeding the admonition given by Isaiah to "enlarge the place of thy tent, and let them stretch forth the curtains of thine habitations: spare not, lengthen thy cords, and strengthen thy stakes" (Isa 54:2, KJV).[29]

As the Mormons continued to expand from Salt Lake City into other regions of the United States and beyond, they believed that they were representing not only the true faith of God but the faith of America. Because America plays such a central role in Mormon theology and because Mormonism was founded there, in many ways it can correctly claim to be truly the most American of religions. The irony for Mormons is that they have nevertheless been, and continue to be, perceived with suspicion and reservations by the American public.

American Theodemocracy

Although the Mormons have always perceived themselves as genuine American patriots, their compatriots have not returned the sentiment. Unlike the immigrants who came to the United States as a promised land in which they could practice their own religion and improve their material life, Mormons had to flee the United States to establish their own Zion. The Mormons' continual move west—from New York to Kirtland, Ohio; Independence, Missouri; and Nauvoo, Illinois—until they reached the Utah Territory was prompted by the religious prejudice and persecution of Americans when Mormons began to become a majority in their communities.[30] Led by Brigham Young, who succeeded Smith, the Mormons reached the Salt Lake Valley in July 1847, where they established a headquarters for migrants who were to follow.[31]

Throughout the nineteenth century, Utah was not the only destination for Mormon migrants. Missionaries were sent to establish settlements in Idaho, Arizona, Nevada, and California.[32] Perhaps the most famous Mormon missionary outpost in the West was in Las Vegas, where Brigham Young assigned William Bringhurst with thirty missionaries to convert the Paiute population.[33] A fort was built near downtown Las Vegas to serve as a stopover for travelers to San Bernardino. Although the Mormons abandoned Las Vegas in 1857, they were able to establish a presence in the intermountain region known today as the "Mormon Corridor," the "Book of Mormon Belt," or the "Jell-O Belt" (the last name was given because of Mormons' reputed affinity for Jell-O—the Utah State Legislature even adopted Jell-O as the official state snack in 2001).[34] Like the South's "Bible Belt," this region, extending from western Wyoming and eastern Idaho down to San Bernardino and Mesa, Arizona, is culturally and religiously homogeneous.[35]

Like the *Mayflower* Pilgrims, who were concerned about losing their cultural identity, the Mormons founded a "theodemocracy" in the Utah Territory, which they named the state of Deseret.[36] Mormon political theory, originated by Joseph Smith and put into successful practice by Brigham Young, fused the republican democratic rights of the U.S. Constitution with Mormon theological beliefs and practices. Believing the Second Coming of Christ was imminent, Smith described this political system as one in which God and people ruled in righteousness for the literal fulfillment of Christ's prayer in the Gospel of Matthew, "Thy kingdom come. Thy will be done in earth, as it is in heaven."[37] However, the law that God gave to his people was in harmony with the republican principles of the U.S. Constitution.[38] Although God was the ultimate power, the daily activities of government were left to mortals to administer among themselves.

This amalgamation of American constitutionalism and Mormon theology was not only unique but also raised questions about the proper relationship between church and state in American civilization. The American public, out of a fear that republican principles would disappear under a theocracy, rejected fusing church and state together; but Smith's political theory was different in advocating a theocracy that was in principle republican. An example of how theodemocracy worked was Smith's Council of Fifty at Nauvoo, which served as a central political authority for the various branches and offices spread across the United States.[39] The council was led by Smith but included prominent non-Mormon members, with full consensus required to pass any measure.[40] Debate was encouraged among all members of the council, and if consensus was not reached, Smith would seek divine revelation to resolve the impasse.

Although theodemocracy sought to minimize faction by promoting consensus, it was never meant to be imposed upon those who were unwilling or non-Mormon. In fact, Smith believed that a religiously plural society would continue to exist even after Christ's return to earth and that therefore theodemocracy required non-Mormon representation.[41] As James T. McHugh states, Mormon theology is "comfortable with . . . [the] human-centric vision of both the Protestant Reformation and the liberal Enlightenment."[42] Being at the center of this theology, moral agency was not only esteemed but became one of the fundamental freedoms for all citizens in Smith's theodemocracy. This makes perfect sense because theodemocracy is a political system separate from the social system of Zion, where the righteous, that is, the LDS Church, associate together.[43] Although the same leaders ruled both secular and ecclesiastical institutions, these roles and their respective organizations were seen as distinct and separate. Zion was an ideal, and theodemocracy a necessity.

Although Americans rejected Smith's theodemocracy and drove the Mormons west to Utah, it was successfully implemented by Brigham Young in the new proposed state of Deseret, which was centered in the Great Basin encompassing all of Utah and Nevada and including large portions of California and Arizona and parts of Colorado, New Mexico, Wyoming, Idaho, and Oregon.[44] In the isolation of the West, the Mormons established a new form of republican government mandated directly by God.

As the United States expanded west it surrounded the Utah Territory. As a result, the Mormons sought to be admitted to the union while remaining true to their theological and political principles. Learning that both California and New Mexico had applied for statehood, Brigham Young sent his application to the federal government in 1849, with a state constitution modeled after that of

Iowa, where the Mormons had temporarily settled on their west-ward migration.[45] Designed to avoid disputes from existing settle-ments, the proposal excluded, for example, Northern California, with its growing population due to the Gold Rush.

Because of the proposal's sheer ambition as well as reservations about the Mormon practice of polygamy, it was not recognized by Congress.[46] In the absence of other authority, the provisional gov-ernment of Deseret became the de facto government of the Great Basin, with a bicameral legislature established, judges appointed, and a criminal code adopted.[47] The LDS Church became incorpo-rated and a militia was formed. The state of Deseret, never recog-nized by the U.S. government, was eclipsed in September of 1850 when it became the Utah Territory by an Act of Congress as part of the Compromise of 1850.[48] Brigham Young was inaugurated as the first governor of the Utah Territory, and on April 4, 1851, the General Assembly of Deseret passed a resolution to dissolve the state of Deseret.

Mormons, however, did not relinquish the idea of the state of Deseret, with its theodemocratic government, until the first trans-continental railroad in 1869, which opened the territory to large numbers of non-Mormons. Prior to this, a group of Mormon lead-ers under Young's leadership continued to meet as a shadow gov-ernment after each session of the territorial legislature to ratify the new laws under the name of the state of Deseret. Multiple attempts were even made in 1856, 1862, and 1872 to write a new state constitution under the name of Deseret, based on the boundar-ies of the Utah Territory.[49] However, none of these attempts were successful.

The Mormon War

In spite of their success in proselytizing the West and securing territorial status, the Mormons continued to face conflict with the U.S. government, which culminated in the Mormon War

(May 1857–July 1858). Offended by polygamy, the U.S. government was also concerned about Brigham Young's theodemocratic
rule in the Utah Territory as federal appointees came into conflict
with the Utah territorial leadership.[50] Although some federal officials maintained harmonious relationships with the Mormons, others did not and were prejudiced against them.[51]

Furthermore, some Mormons were scornful of federal rule
over their territory, especially without their having a say over their
appointment.[52] Although Mormons declared their loyalty to the
United States and celebrated the Fourth of July, they were critical of the federal government because it offered them no compas-
sion after they had been driven out of their homes in the Northeast
and Midwest. The Mormons also used the system of ecclesiastical courts rather than federal ones when dealing with civil matters
like marriage, land titles, and water rights. The result was a state
of constant tension and conflict between the federal officials who
were appointed as overlords of the Utah Territory and the Mormons, who remembered their past experiences with the United
States and resented being ruled again by a people who viewed them
with prejudice and who were unaccountable for perceived wrongs.

The Mormons therefore posed two challenges to American
civilization in their understanding of the relationships between
church and state and between the territories and the federal government. With their ecclesiastical courts, Mormons practiced
a jurisprudence that was contrary to that in the other states and
territories. Although this practice was consistent with theodemocratic principles, it struck many Americans, especially federal officials who lived in the state, as unconstitutional and un-American.
Furthermore, these officials opposed polygamy and believed it was
the role of the federal government to intervene in a matter traditionally reserved for the states and territories.

The specific event that precipitated the Mormon War was
the claim of a number of federal officials in Utah that their safety
was in danger. These "runaway officials"—Territorial Secretary

Broughton Harris and Judges Perry Brocchus and Lemuel Bran-
denbury—had serious disagreements with the Mormons about the
practice of polygamy. Another judge, William W. Drummond,
resigned from the Utah Territorial Supreme Court because he
claimed that the Mormons ignored the laws of Congress and the
Constitution. He urged the president to appoint a non-Mormon
governor and send with him sufficient military aid to enforce the
laws of the United States.[53] Chief Justice Kinney also cited Young's
perversion of the Utah judicial system and seconded Drummond's
suggestion.[54]

Although President Buchanan did not investigate these charges,
under popular and political pressure he decided to take decisive
action against the Mormons, who were thought to be in a state
of rebellion against the United States. First Buchanan appointed
the non-Mormon Alfred Cumming to take Young's place as governor; and second, he sent twenty-five hundred army troops to build
a post in Utah and act as a posse comitatus once Cumming was
installed.[55] They were ordered not to take offensive action against
the Mormons but to defend themselves if attacked. Fearing that
the troops had been sent to annihilate them, the Mormons blocked
their entrance into the Salt Lake Valley and activated the Nauvoo
Legion, the Mormon militia. The two military forces made first
contact in late September 1857 in southwestern Wyoming.[56] The
actual fighting was slight: the Mormon militia raided the army
supply trains, and in the one exchange where bullets were fired,
nobody was killed or injured. The Mormons were able to protect the passages into the Salt Lake City, while U.S. army waited
through the winter of 1857 and 1858 for new supplies. Governor
Cumming sent a proclamation to the citizens of Utah declaring
them to be in rebellion, and a grand jury was later formed that
indicted Brigham Young and over sixty other members of the Mormon leadership for treason.[57]

Brigham Young wrote to Thomas L. Kane of Pennsylvania, an
attorney and military officer of some prominence who had helped

the Mormons in their westward migration, to assist them.[58] Kane, in turn, wrote to Buchanan offering to mediate between the Mormons and the U.S. government. In the previous year's State of the Union address, Buchanan had taken a hard stance against the Mormon rebellion, but now he feared that Mormons might defeat the Utah Expedition at great political cost to himself. He stated that he would pardon the Mormons if they would submit to the U.S. government's authority, and he granted Kane unofficial permission to attempt meditation. Kane traveled to the Utah Territory and met with Young, who agreed to accept Buchanan's appointment of Cumming as territorial governor. Kane then met with the Utah Expedition force and persuaded Cumming to travel to Salt Lake City without military escort under the guarantee of safe conduct. Cumming was received by Young and the Mormons in mid-April and shortly thereafter was installed as the new territorial governor.

Despite Kane's successful mission, the two sides still regarded each other with suspicion throughout the spring and summer of 1858. Although he accepted Cumming as governor, Young feared he would be persecuted if the army was allowed to enter Utah. Young decided at the end of winter to evacuate the Utah Territory and move to Nevada, and to burn the capital city of Salt Lake to the ground, rather than directly confront the U.S. army.[59] In the meantime, Buchanan, under pressure from Congress to end the crisis, sent an official peace commission to Utah. The commission, which arrived in June, offered free pardons to Mormons for any acts related to the conflict if they would submit to U.S. governmental authority, including the Utah Expedition.[60] The U.S. government would not interfere with their religion, and the commission suggested that, while U.S. troops would remain, their presence would be reduced and they would protect people from the Native Americans and ensure the passage of emigrants to California. Young accepted Buchanan's terms, although he denied Utah was ever in a state of rebellion. The result was a war with no battles, few casualties, and resolved by negotiation.

The biggest casualties of the Mormon War were non-Mormon civilians in what is known as the Mountain Meadow massacre on September 11, 1857.[61] Arkansas emigrants passing through the Utah Territory were attacked by the Mormon militia, who were dressed as Native Americans, and a small contingent of Paiute tribesmen. Approximately 120 men, women, and children were slaughtered, with only 17 children under the age of eight spared. Only one person, John D. Lee, was tried in a court of law, convicted, and sentenced to death. This incident continues to draw controversy as to whether Brigham Young was directly involved. The LDS Church excommunicated some of the participants in the massacre in 1872 and has acknowledged the involvement of local Mormon leaders.

Both the Mormons and the U.S. government had achieved peace, but the Mormons had fared worse. Nominally under military occupation, the Mormons lived in peaceful but tense coexistence with the U.S. troops until they left in 1861 for the Civil War.[62] The Republican-controlled Congress subsequently passed the Morrill Anti-Bigamy Act (1862).[63] Lacking control of the executive branch and the federal district courts, the Mormons still were able to maintain political authority in the Territorial Legislature and the probate court system. But a series of events would end Mormon isolation after the Mormon War: the completion of the transcontinental railroad in 1869, which brought in large numbers of non-Mormon residents; Utah's successful application for statehood in 1896; and the completion of the Smoot hearings in 1907.[64]

Besides the Native Americans and the Southern States, Mormons were the only organized group that went to war with the federal government within the United States. Although not anywhere near the size and scale of the American Civil War or the American-Indian Wars, the Mormon War did settle the matter of polygamy, church-state relations, and the role of the federal government in the internal affairs of a state or territory. In this sense, it was similar to those conflicts in that it took military action to decide the questions at stake.

The American Narrative

By the midpoint of the twentieth century, the Mormon Church had effectively put polygamy and much of its peculiar culture behind it. Some argue that thanks in part to new leadership and a growing emphasis on family and study of the Bible in church meetings, the typical Mormon values of the 1950s were aligned with those of mainstream America.[65] God, family, and country provided a foundation of faith for both Mormons and the majority of American Christians. Businesses found that Mormons were profitable employees, dedicated to hard work, and loyal. At the same time, Church leaders in Utah encouraged Mormon youth to leave the Mountain West to study at some of the best schools in the nation, thereby making a name for the Church in scholarly circles.[66] Additionally, the growing population of Mormons in Utah and their out-migration to distant states "contributed to the ongoing Mormon reintegration with America and led to the establishment of major Mormon outposts on the two American coasts."[67]

As American mainstream culture has become more secular and fragmented since the 1960s, Mormons have become aligned with the socially and politically conservative side of the culture. However, this social and politically conservative alignment does not make Mormons less American than other conservatives; rather, it places them as full participants in an ongoing debate about what constitutes American culture and politics. The beliefs and practices that caused difficulties for Mormons in the past in being accepted as Americans are no longer considered legitimate points for their opponents to use against them. And yet Mormons are still not entirely accepted by mainstream America. While they are undisputedly Americans, questions arise as to whether their religion is Christian, whether their Church has political ambitions, and whether their candidates should be president.

From its humble beginnings in rural New York State, the Mormon Church has become a worldwide organization with over 13 million members.[68] There is something truly American in this pull-yourself-up-by-your-bootstraps kind of determination and eventual success. Mormonism therefore is the "theology of Americanism."[69] As such, it is more than simply a religious outgrowth of the Jacksonian-American ethos. In a speech given during a presidential visit to Salt Lake City, John F. Kennedy suggested that more than being a derivative of the American story, the story of Mormonism might actually be an inspiration to it. Speaking of the "rags-to-riches" achievement of the Church, he said,

> The Mormons of a century ago were a persecuted and prosecuted minority, harried from place to place, the victims of violence and occasionally murder, while today, in the short space of 100 years, their faith and works are known and respected the world around, and their voices heard in the highest councils of this country. . . . *As the Mormons succeeded, so America can succeed*, if we will not give up or turn our back.[70]

CONCLUSION
The Most American of Religions

After reviewing the contributions that Mormonism has made to American civilization in such areas as popular culture, national politics, and social controversies, one could argue that Mormonism is the most American of all of the American religions—not only because it is indigenous to this country and cedes a special place to America in its theology, but also because it both confirms and challenges the core values of American civilization, thereby situating itself in a unique position as both an affirmer and questioner of America itself. Although all religions in America have played, to some extent, the role of both defender and critic of this country, Mormonism has done so from the very beginning of its existence and continues to do so today, as attested by the fact that Mormons are still received with alternating acceptance and suspicion from the American public.

Mixed reviews on the role of Mormonism in American culture may be clearly found in popular culture, where Mormons are often portrayed as representing both the familiar and the bizarre: the all-American values of family and church and the secretive culture of mysterious temples and the past practice of polygamy. Through these various interpretive lenses, Mormonism is shown to simultaneously affirm and critique mainstream American values, thereby exposing the tension inherent in them. The resulting popular sentiment is mix of admiration for the material success and social wholesomeness of the LDS and a fascination with the seemingly strange and inscrutable beliefs and practices they hold sacred. The increasing presence of Mormons in popular culture serves to educate the public on the nuances of LDS life while raising important questions regarding what it means to be American.

Among the important cultural questions brought forward in this exchange is that of the role and function of marriage in the United States. Historically, with its revelation and practice of polygamy, Mormons challenged the American conception of monogamous marriage as well as other jurisprudential areas like church-state relations and federalism. When the Utah Territory applied for statehood, these issues became front and center in the national conversation and in the evolving definition of American civilization. Remarkably, despite a general national commitment to both religious and individual freedom, it was necessary for the LDS Church to renounce the practice of polygamy, remove church involvement in secular affairs, and accept federal intervention in a state matter in order to become accepted into the union. Through these actions, they demonstrated their willingness to become American and helped to clarify precisely what that meant. In many ways, these accommodations to the nation were a conscientious step toward Mormonism becoming the American religion: whereas they had once challenged the American concept of marriage, family, and government, they now accept and promote them.

Still, the Mormons' promotion of American values has not resulted in full acceptance into American civilization. Remaining apprehensions on the part of the public at large are evident in the mistrustful treatment of Mormon politicians, particularly those who run for the presidency. The irony is that these apprehensions—about Mormons' intolerance, their social homogeneity, and their religion—actually reflect the American public's own religious intolerance and disregard for social pluralism. Americans project their own fears and prejudices upon the Mormons, a group about which they know little and which, despite its continued efforts to embrace and embody all that is American, remains outside the mainstream.

Continued reservations about Mormons, as manifested in popular culture and politics, often stem from arguments surrounding the LDS conception of Christianity and reveal the continuing importance of Christianity in defining the cultural foundations of American civilization. By challenging the accepted parameters of what it means to be Christian in America—particularly in their source of revelation and their understanding of the role of Christ and America's place in Christian theology—Mormons have indirectly questioned the religio-cultural foundations of America. This challenge has not gone unnoticed by the mainstream, and has been met at alternate times with prejudice, reservations, and partial acceptance. Whether the current relationship of accommodation and simultaneous suspicion between Mormons and Americans at large will ever change depends heavily on whether Americans can ever accept Mormonism as legitimately and fully Christian.

As an experiment in democracy, America continues to evolve into something new, with its core values being defined and redefined over time. Certain values, such as Christianity or marriage, are constantly being defended, challenged, and changed as American civilization adapts to new circumstances in its development, whether the conquering of the western frontier, assimilating mass immigration, coping with societal industrialization, or becoming a global power. The history of the Mormons in America follows this same pattern of adapting to new situations, as they have defended their religion and culture when challenged and made accommodations in an effort to make a place for themselves in American civilization. Unlike other religious groups, Mormons already lived in America before they had to leave it, and later, when they had no choice, they returned back to it. In the unique position of desiring to become American even though they are from America, Mormons have been able to contribute to defining American civilization. In this sense, Mormonism is not only the most American of religions, but it is the religion of America itself.

NOTES

Introduction

1   Charles William Eliot, "Five American Contributions to Civilization," in *The Oxford Book of American Essays*, ed. Brander Matthews (Oxford: Oxford University Press, 1914), 208–307; Arthur M. Schlesinger Sr., "Our Ten Contributions to Civilization," *Atlantic*, March 1959, 65–69; Claude Fischer, *Made in America: A Social History of American Culture and Character* (Chicago: University of Chicago Press, 2010). Other works to consult about American civilization are Roderick Nash, *Wilderness and the American Mind* (New Haven: Yale University Press, 1982); Leo Marx, *The Machine in the Garden* (Oxford: Oxford University Press, 2000); Alexis de Tocqueville, *Democracy in America* (Chicago: University of Chicago Press, 2002); David Hollinger, *The American Intellectual Tradition*, 4th ed., 2 vols. (Oxford: Oxford University Press, 2001–5).

2   For more information regarding the origin and content of the Book of Mormon, refer to chapter 4.

3   J. Gordon Melton, *Encyclopedia of American Religions*, 7th ed. (Farmington Hills, Mich.: Thomson Gale, 2002).

Chapter 1

1   For more about Donny's professional career, refer to Donny.com, http://www.donny.com/.

2   Steve Burgess, "Donny Osmond: We Suffer for His Art," Salon.com, September 21, 1999, accessed April 1, 2010, http://www.salon.com/people/feature/1999/09/21/osmond/index.html.

3   "Donny Osmond," BBC News, December 6, 2004, http://news.bbc.co.uk/2/hi/programmes/hardtalk/4054629.stm. In the interview, Michael Jackson suggests to Donny Osmond that he change his name because it is considered too wholesome.

4   For example, refer to the following television reviews: Heather Havrilesky, I Like to Watch, Salon.com, March 5, 2006, accessed April 1, 2010, http://www.salon.com/entertainment/iltw/2006/03/05/big_love/index.html; Maureen Ryan, "It's Hard Out Here for a Polygamist: 'Big Love,'" Chicago Tribune, March 9, 2006, accessed April 1, 2010, http://featuresblogs.chicagotribune.com/entertainment_tv/big_love/; James Poniewozik, "Top Ten Returning TV Series," Time, December 9, 2009, accessed April 1, 2010, http://www.time.com/time/specials/2007/article/0,28804,1686204_1686244_1691404,00.html.

5   LDS Church, "Church Responds to Questions on HBO's Big Love," Newsroom of the Church of Jesus Christ of Latter-day Saints, March 6, 2006, http://newsroom.lds.org/ldsnewsroom/eng/commentary/church-responds-to-questions-on-hbo-s-big-love.

6   Quoted in Ben Wilson, "LDS Church Rejects Polygamous Accusations," Deseret News, February 28, 2006, http://www.deseretnews.com/article/1,5143,635188091,00.html.

7   LDS Church, "The Publicity Dilemma," Newsroom of the Church of Jesus Christ of the Latter-Day Saints, March 9, 2009, http://newsroom.lds.org/ldsnewsroom/eng/commentary/the-publicity-dilemma.

8   For a negative review of this episode, refer to Chris Hicks, "TV Portrayal of Mormons Mean, Callous," Deseret Morning News, June 5, 2005, accessed April 1, 2010, http://www.deseretnews.com/article1,5143,600131613,00.html.

9   The episode where Mormonism is explicitly commented on is "Tea and Sympathy," which first aired on May 1, 2007.

10 For more about these participants, refer to CBS, Survivor, http://www.cbs.com/primetime/survivor/.

11 In fact, she was so popular that she was invited to appear in two episodes of MTV's reality show Road Rules.

12 Sally Atkinson, "America's Next Top Mormon, Reality-TV Shows Are

Plucking Contestants from an Unlikely Pew," *Newsweek*, May 19, 2008, accessed April 1, 2010, http://www.newsweek.com/id/136340.

13   Atkinson, "America's Next Top Mormon."

14   For more about Ken Jennings and his endorsements, refer to Ken Jennings, Confessions of a Trivial Mind, http://www.ken-jennings.com/aboutken .html.

15   Ken Jennings, "Politicians and Pundits, Please Stop Slandering My Mormon Faith,"*New York Daily News*, December 18, 2007, accessed April 1, 2010, http:// www.nydailynews.com/opinions/2007/12/19/2007-12-19_politicians _pundits_please_stop_slander.html.

16   Steve Evans, "South Park Mormonism," *Dialogue*, June 3, 2006, accessed April 1, 2010, http://bycommonconsent.com/2006/06/03/south-park-mormonism/. The South Park creators, Terry Parker and Matt Stone, have teamed up with Robert Lopez to create the latest commercial and critical hit on Broadway, *The Book of Mormon*. In this musical Mormons are portrayed sympathetically and satirically but, in the words of one critic, "by the end of the evening—strangely enough—no offense has been given and no damage has been done. . . ." James Fenton, "The Saints Take Broadway," *New York Review of Books*, July 14, 2011, accessed on July 11, 2011: http://www.nybooks.com/articles/archives/2011/jul/14/saints-take -broadway/.

17   James E. Ford, "Battlestar Galatica and Mormon Theology." *Journal of Popular Culture* 17 (1983): 83–87.

18   Ford, "Battlestar Galatica."

19   Ellen Leventry, "Born-Again 'Battle Star,'" *Beliefnet*, http://www.beliefnet .com/Entertainment/Movies/2005/05/Born-Again-Battlestar.aspx.

20   Richard L. Bushman, *Joseph Smith and the Beginnings of Mormonism* (Urbana: University of Illinois Press, 1984), 170.

21   This is not to equate the violence Mormons suffered with the prejudicial treatment homosexuals experience, but rather to show the similarities in how two minority groups were treated by the majority of Americans. For more about violence against Mormons, refer to Jan Shipps, *Mormonism: The Story of a Religious Tradition* (Urbana: University of Illinois Press, 1985), 155–61.

22   The tagline for Beck's program on Fox News is "The fusion of entertainment and enlightenment."

23   Beck's show first hit number one in the ratings in September 2009 and has consistently been among the three highest-rated cable news shows.

24   *An Inconvenient Book* in 2007, *The Christmas Sweater* in 2008, *Arguing with Idiots*, and a children's picture version of *The Christmas Sweater* in 2009. Beck

is also the author of *Glenn Beck's Common Sense: The Case Against an Out-of-control Government* (2009), and *The Real America* (2003).

25 Joel Campbell, "Focus on Family Pulls Glenn Beck Article," *Mormon Times*, December 27, 2008, accessed April 1, 2010, http://www.mormontimes .com/mormon_voices/joel_campbell/?id=5597.

26 In response to this controversy, Beck posted a "special commentary" on his website, pleading for religious tolerance. "At a time when the world is so full of fear, despair, and divisions," he says, "it is my hope that all of those who believe in a loving and peaceful God would stand together on the universal message of hope and forgiveness." "Glenn Beck Story Pulled Because of His Mormon Faith," *The Glenn Beck Program*, January 4, 2009, http://www.glennbeck.com/content/articles/article/200/19594/.

27 Some would argue that this is because Beck does not promote his Mormonism openly. For instance, a DVD produced by LDS-affiliated Deseret Book entitled *Glenn Beck: An Unlikely Mormon* is not advertised on his website. Of course, there are detractors. Notable among them is Stephen King, who in 2007 referred to Beck as "Satan's mentally challenged younger brother." "Television Impaired," *Entertainment Weekly*, February 1, 2007, accessed April 1, 2010, http://www.ew.com/ew/article/0,,20008933,00.html.

28 As he refers to them in his 2003 book.

29 Beck cites Skousen in *The Real America* (2003) and has promoted his work on the air.

30 Joanna Brooks, "How Mormonism Built Glenn Beck," *Religious Dispatches*, October 27, 2009, accessed April 1, 2010, http://www.religiondispatches .org/archive/religiousright/1885/how_mormonism_built_glenn_ beck?page=entire.

31 David Von Drehle, "Mad Man: Is Glenn Beck Bad for America?" *Time*, September 17, 2009, accessed April 1, 2010, http://www.time.com/time/ politics/article/0,8599,1924348,00.html.

32 Refer to chapter 3 of this book.

33 Huckabee is also on Fox News, filling a Sunday evening time slot.

34 They even have their own annual LDS Film Festival.

35 Interestingly, Dutcher is no longer a practicing Mormon and no longer makes Mormon films. He announced his departure from the faith and his lament over the current state of Mormon filmmaking (he says some films are frankly "not very good") in an open letter published in the *Provo Daily Herald*. He also stated his lingering hope: "Wouldn't it be amazing," he said, "if the Mormon community did what nobody else in the world seems interested in doing: exploring human spirituality, human truth in film. Expand the vocabulary of film, learn to do things on the broad white canvas of a movie screen that no one has yet imagined." Richard Dutcher, "Richard Dutcher:

'Parting Words' on Mormon Movies," *Daily Herald*, April 11, 2007, accessed April 1, 2010, http://www.heraldextra.com/news/opinion/utah-valley/article_c07f4ae0-bbee-5265-89c1-bae7b12ce676.html.
36 Information provided at the film's website, http://saintsandsoldiers.com/.
37 Spencer Kimball, "First Presidency Message: The Gospel Vision of the Arts," *Ensign*, July 1977, 3.
38 Including four Teen Choice Awards.
39 February 2, 2010. These are markers of a faithful LDS lifestyle.
40 Michael Barrier, "Bluth Talk," http://www.michaelbarrier.com/Home%20Page/WhatsNewArchivesApril09.htm#bluthtalk, April 6, 2009.
41 Amy K. Stewart, "BYU Center to Develop Animation Creations," *Deseret News*, March 28, 2008, accessed April 1, 2008, http://www.deseretnews.com/article/1,5143,695265400,00.html.
42 Kimball, "First Presidency Message."
43 Because Deseret Book is a for-profit company privately owned by the LDS Church, no sales figures are made available to the public.
44 "About Deseret Book Company," accessed March 5, 2010, http://deseretbook.com/about.
45 Ethan Thomas, "'Twilight' Loses Luster with Deseret Book," *Deseret News*, April 23, 2010, accessed April 1, 2010, http://www.deseretnews.com/article/705299108/Twilight-loses-luster-with-Deseret-Book.html.
46 "The Top 100 Titles of 2008," *USA Today*, January 14, 2009, http://www.usatoday.com/life/books/news/2009-01-14-top-100-titles_N.htm.
47 Stephenie Meyer, "Bio," accessed March 5, 2010, http://www.stepheniemeyer.com/bio.html.
48 "The 2009 Celebrity 100," *Forbes*, June 3, 2009, http://www.forbes.com/lists/2009/53/celebrity-09_Stephenie-Meyer_NORR.html. Also "The 2008 Time 100 Finalists," *Time*, accessed March 5, 2010, http://www.time.com/time/specials/2007/article/0,28804,1725112_1726934_1726935,00.html.
49 Tony-Allen Mills, "News Review Interview: Stephenie Meyer," *Sunday Times*, August 10, 2008, accessed April 1, 2010, http://entertainment.timesonline.co.uk/tol/arts_and_entertainment/books/article4492238.ece.
50 Lev Grossman, "Stephenie Meyer: A New J. K. Rowling?" *Time*, April 24, 2008, accessed April 1, 2010, http://www.time.com/time/magazine/article/0,9171,1734838,00.html#ixzz0gT11bdmP.
51 Grossman, "Stephenie Meyer."
52 The Nebula Award (1985–86) and the Hugo Award (1986–87). Never before or since have the awards been given to the same author in two consecutive years.

53 "Orson Scott Card Interview," Hatrack River, the Official Website of Orson Scott Card, accessed March 5, 2010, http://www.hatrack.com/research/interviews/interview.shtml.

54 Stephen R. Covey, "About Stephen R. Covey," accessed March 5, 2010, https://www.stephencovey.com/about/about.php.

55 Stephen R. Covey, *The Divine Center* (Salt Lake City: Deseret Book, 2005), 240.

56 "Share with Us How The 7 Habits Has Changed Your Life," Franklin-Covey Blog, March 14, 2009, http://www.franklincovey.com/blog/20th-anniversary-7-habits-highly-effective-people.html.

Chapter 2

1 Armand Mauss, *The Angel and the Beehive: The Mormon Struggle with Assimilation* (Urbana: University of Illinois Press, 1994).

2 Nancy F. Cott, *Public Vows: A History of Marriage and the Nation* (Cambridge, Mass.: Harvard University Press, 2000); Ellis Sandoz, *Republicanism, Religion, and the Soul of America* (Columbia: University of Missouri Press, 2006).

3 Montesquieu makes this equation explicit in his other famous work, *The Spirit of the Laws*.

4 William Paley, *The Principles of Moral and Political Philosophy* (Boston: Benj. Mussey, 1853).

5 Cott, *Public Vows*.

6 Some "Mormons" who are not members of the Church of Jesus Christ of Latter-day Saints (such as fundamentalists) continue to practice polygamy today, despite the threat of state prosecution.

7 Reports suggest that Smith received revelation on polygamy and practiced it as early as 1831. Fawn M. Brodie, *No Man Knows My History: The Life of Joseph Smith* (New York: Vintage, 1995); Richard L. Bushman, *Joseph Smith.: A Rough Stone Rolling* (New York: Vintage, 2007).

8 Bushman, *Joseph Smith: A Rough Stone Rolling*.

9 Joseph Smith's revelations from God are recorded in *Doctrine and Covenants*, a book revered as scripture by members of the LDS Church. This particular quotation comes from *Doctrine and Covenants* 132:61–62.

10 Bushman, *Joseph Smith: A Rough Stone Rolling*.

11 Whitney Cross, *The Burned-over District: The Social and Intellectual History of Enthusiastic Religion in Western New York, 1800–1850* (Ithaca: Cornell University Press, 1950).

12 Nathan Hatch, *The Democratization of American Christianity* (New Haven, Conn.: Yale University Press, 1991).

13 In order for families to be reunited after death, they must be sealed together in sacred ceremonies. Part of the ritual of sealing (joining) families together takes place in Mormon temples. Unlike regular meeting-houses (which are used for Sunday worship and activities throughout the week), temples are dedicated to a higher purpose, and access to them is restricted to those who have been interviewed and found worthy to enter by their local and regional Church authorities. In them, marriage ceremonies are performed "for time and all eternity" rather than "until death do us part."

14 These are twentieth-century justifications and are most clearly argued by offshoot branches of the LDS Church. For example, the Strangite movement explains that polygamy is actually a liberating practice for women. The Original Church of Jesus Christ of Latter Day Saints, "Women," accessed January 18, 2010, http://www.strangite.org/Women.htm.

15 Leonard J. Arrington, *Great Basin Kingdom: An Economic History of the Latter-day Saints, 1830–1900*, 3rd ed. (Urbana: University of Illinois Press, 2004).

16 Enemies of the Mormons did petition the government to reject the Deseret proposal, citing what they characterized as unpatriotic temple oaths and lasting animosities between the LDS and the national government arising from the ill treatment they had received in the East and the murder of their founding prophet. Furthermore, because much of the proposed territory of the state of Deseret would have come from what had been Mexican territory only a year before, or under British control in recent memory, the U.S. government could not take the chance of having a group with questionably loyalty to the union in charge of its political affairs. Arrington, *Great Basin Kingdom*.

17 Linda Thatcher, "Statehood Chronology," Online Utah, accessed January 14, 2008, http://www.onlineutah.com/statehoodchronology.shtml.

18 As part of a compromise meant to prevent the Civil War conflict, there was no mention of slavery.

19 To thank Millard Fillmore for his kindness, Utah has both a county (Millard) and a city (Fillmore) named after him. Michael Kent Winder, *Presidents and Prophets: The Story of America's Presidents and the LDS Church* (American Fork, Utah: Covenant Communications, 2007).

20 O. Kendall White, "Mormonism in America and Canada: Accommodation to Nation-State," *Canadian Journal of Sociology–Cahiers Canadiens de Sociologie* 3, no. 2 (1978): 161–81.

21 D. L. Bigler, *Forgotten Kingdom: The Mormon Theocracy in the American West, 1847–1896* (Logan: Utah State University Press, 1998); William P.

MacKinnon, ed., *At Sword's Point: A Documentary History of the Utah War to 1858* (Norman: University of Oklahoma Press, 2008).

22 The Fourteenth Amendment was adopted in 1868 and incorporated the First Amendment's Establishment and Free Exercise Clauses to apply to the states. Prior to the Fourteenth Amendment, the regulation of church-state relations was reserved to the states.

23 Robert Alley, *The Constitution and Religion: Leading Supreme Court Cases on Church and State* (Amherst, N.Y.: Prometheus Books, 1999), 414–19.

24 The Act also disenfranchised Utah women, who had been given the right to vote in 1870.

25 Alley, *Constitution and Religion*.

26 This announcement, made in a letter to the general church audience, is included in LDS Scripture along with *Doctrine and Covenants* and is known as *Official Declaration 1*.

27 Richard S. Van Wagoner, *Mormon Polygamy: A History* (Salt Lake City: Signature Books, 1989). For more about Taylor's religious experience with polygamy, also refer to Martha Sonntag Bradley, *Kidnapped from That Land: The Government Raids on the Short Creek Polygamists* (Salt Lake City: University of Utah Press, 1993); and Ken Driggs, "After the Manifesto: Modern Polygamy and Fundamentalist Mormons," *Journal of Church and State* 32 (1990): 367–89; for more about Lorin Woolley and his father, John, refer to Ben Bradlee Jr. and Dale Van Atta, *Prophet of Blood: The Untold Story of Ervil LeBaron and the Lambs of God* (New York: Putnam, 1981).

28 Hans A. Baer, *Recreating Utopia in the Desert: A Sectarian Challenge to Modern Mormonism* (Albany: State University of New York Press, 1988); Bradley, *Kidnapped from That Land*; Van Wagoner, *Mormon Polygamy*.

29 Bradley, *Kidnapped from That Land*.

30 Van Wagoner, *Mormon Polygamy*; refer to article 3 of the 1896 Utah Constitution; chapter 112, section 103-51-2 of the Utah Penal Code, and chapter 7, section 76-7-101 of the Utah Criminal Code.

31 Bradlee and Van Atta, *Prophet of Blood*; Van Wagoner, *Mormon Polygamy*.

32 Bradlee and Van Atta, *Prophet of Blood*; Bradley, *Kidnapped from That Land*; Van Wagoner, *Mormon Polygamy*.

33 Ken Driggs, "Who Shall Raise the Children? Vera Black and the Rights of Polygamous Utah Parents," *Utah Historical Quarterly* 60 (1992): 27; also see Driggs, "After the Manifesto."

34 For example, "The Great Love-Nest Raid," *Time*, March 8, 1953; "People: The Big Raid," *Newsweek*, March 8, 1953; also see Van Wagoner, *Mormon Polygamy*.

35 Bradley, *Kidnapped from That Land*.

36 Irwin Altman and Joseph Grant, *Polygamous Families in Contemporary Societies* (Cambridge: Cambridge University Press, 1996), 50–53.

37 Sara Corbett, "Children of God," *The New York Times*, July 27, 2008. Also refer to "Timeline of Raid on FLDS-Owned YFZ Ranch," *Deseret News*, May 23, 2008.

38 Ben Winslow, "Jeffs Is Now an Inmate at Utah State Prison," *Deseret News*, November 22, 2007. However, after his release, Jeffs has returned to resume leadership of the FLDS Church.

39 Although Blacks were numbered among LDS Church members from the 1830s, they were not included in the offices of the priesthood (authority given to LDS men to act in God's name and run the church). The specific reasons for this practice are unclear and were not discussed by LDS leadership. Under pressure from civil rights activists in the 1960's, Church leadership explained that it would take a revelation from God (rather than the suggestion of Church members) to change the policy. This revelation came to then Church President Spencer W. Kimball in 1978. Since that time, Black members of the LDS Church are permitted the same rights and privileges of other worthy, practicing members of the faith, including ordination to the priesthood, positions in Church leadership, and participation in temple ceremonies.

40 Altman and Grant, *Polygamous Families*; Bradlee and Van Atta, *Prophet of Blood*; Van Wagoner, *Mormon Polygamy*.

41 Altman and Grant, *Polygamous Families*.

42 Tom Smart, *In Plain Sight: The Startling Truth behind the Elizabeth Smart Investigation* (Chicago: Chicago Review Press, 2005); Jon Krakauer, *Under the Banner of Heaven* (New York: Random House, 2003).

43 Oprah Winfrey, "Polygamy in America," *Oprah*, October 26, 2007.

44 Krakauer, *Under the Banner*; Elissa Wall and Lisa Pulitzer, *Stolen Innocence: My Story of Growing up in a Polygamous Sect, Becoming a Teenage Bride, and Breaking Free of Warren Jeffs* (New York: HarperCollins, 2008).

45 For example, Havrilesky, I Like to Watch.

46 "Church Responds to Questions on HBO's *Big Love*," March 6, 2006, LDS Church's Newsroom, http://newsroom.lds.org/ldsnewsroom/eng/commentary/church-responds-to-questions-on-hbo-s-big-love.

47 Jesse McKinley and Kirk Johnson, "Mormons Tipped Scale in Ban on Gay Marriage," *The New York Times*, November 14, 2008.

48 Tamara Audi, "Mormon Church Backs Salt Lake City's Gay-Right Ordinances," *Wall Street Journal*, November 12, 2009.

49 Not to mention that what often is portrayed as "authentically American" has been described by conservatives, who also are opposed to same-sex marriage. It would make sense for the LDS Church to align itself with

these like-minded groups to be on the side of authenticity as well as for agreement on their public policies.

50 Gordon Hinckley, James Faust, and Thomas Monson, *The Family: A Proclamation to the World,* http://www.lds.org/library/display/0,4945, 161-1-11-1,00.html.

Chapter 3

1 Damon Linker, "The Big Test: Taking Mormonism Seriously," *New Republic,* January 15, 2007, accessed August 1, 2010, http://www.tnr.com/article/politics/the-big-test.

2 Richard Lyman Bushman and Damon Linker, "Mitt Romney's Mormonism: A TNR Online Debate," *New Republic*, January 3–5, 2007, accessed August 1, 2010, http://www.tnr.com/article/politics/mitt-romneys-mormonism.

3 Bushman and Linker, "Mitt Romney's Mormonism."

4 Bushman and Linker, "Mitt Romney's Mormonism."

5 It should come to no surprise that some scholars have paired Mormons and Muslims together as two groups who are not fully accepted in the United States. More of this will be discussed in chapter 4.

6 Robert S. Wicks and Fred R. Foister, *Presidential Politics and the Assassination of the First Mormon Prophet* (Logan: Utah State University Press, 2005), 81–92.

7 Wicks and Foister, *Presidential Politics*, 1.

8 Wicks and Foister, *Presidential Politics*, 1.

9 Wicks and Foister, *Presidential Politics*, 111–22.

10 Wicks and Foister, *Presidential Politics*, 123–31.

11 Wicks and Foister, *Presidential Politics*, 106.

12 For more about the assassination and who is responsible, refer to Wicks and Foister, *Presidential Politics*, 250–84.

13 Theodore H. White, *The Making of the President, 1968* (New York: Atheneum, 1969), 41.

14 White, *Making of the President*, 60–61, 229.

15 \Warren Weaver Jr., "Romney Suddenly Quits; Rockefeller Reaffirms Availability to a Draft," *The New York Times*, February 29, 1968.

16 *National Party Conventions, 1831–2004* (Washington, D.C.: CQ Press, 2005), 131.

17 Robert D. Hershey Jr., "A Family Reunion: Romney, Recalling 1968, Explains It All," *New York Times*, July 6, 1987.

18 Warren Weaver Jr., "Romney Sounds an Uncertain Trumpet," *New York Times Magazine,* November 19, 1967; White, *The Making of the President,*

1968, 56–57; Jules Witcover, *Marathon: The Pursuit of the Presidency, 1972–1976* (New York: Viking Press, 1977), 88.

19 Andrew L. Johns, "Achilles' Heel: The Vietnam War and George Romney's Bid for the Presidency, 1967 to 1968," *Michigan Historical Review* 26 (2000): 1.

20 Johns, "Achilles' Heel," 1.

21 "The Brainwashed Candidate," *Time*, September 15, 1967; Rhodes Cook, "Like Father, Like Son? The Romneys Run for President," Larry J. Sabato's Crystal Ball, September 20, 2007, http://www.centerforpolitics.org/crystalball/articles/frc2007092001/.

22 "The Brainwashed Candidate."

23 Tom Raum, "Presidential Candidates' Religion Playing Big Role in Contest," *Telegraph*, July 31, 2007; Steve Kornacki, "Romney More G.H.W.B. than J.F.K.," *New York Observer*, July 21, 2009. Some contend that Romney's religion would have been more an issue had he been more *successful* in the campaign. Refer to Cook, "Like Father, Like Son?"; and Robert Windeler, "Mormon Leaders Heard by 25,000," *The New York Times*, October 2, 1967.

24 Kimberly H. Conger, "Evangelicals, Issues, and the 2008 Iowa Caucuses," *Politics and Religion* 3 (2010): 130–49; Diane Winston, "Back to the Future: Religion, Politics, and the Media," *American Quarterly* 59, no. 3 (2007): 969–89.

25 Tom Mahoney, *The Story of George Romney: Builder, Salesman, Crusader* (New York: Harper & Brothers, 1960), 3–4, 87.

26 Sidney Fine, *Expanding the Frontier of Civil Rights: Michigan, 1948–1968* (Detroit: Wayne State University Press, 2000), 216–18.

27 Michael Dobbs, "Four Pinocchios for Romney on MLK," *Washington Post*, December 23, 2007.

28 Willis Frederick Dunbar and George S. May, *Michigan: A History of the Wolverine State* (Grand Rapids: Eerdmans, 1995), 584–85 (emphasis in original).

29 Fine, *Expanding the Frontier of Civil Rights*, 335.

30 Paul Brace, *State Government and Economic Performance* (Baltimore: John sHopkins University Press, 1994), 54–55; "Romney Wins Key Test in Fight for Fiscal Reform in Michigan," *The New York Times*, June 29, 1967, 16; Brock Brower, "Puzzling Front Runner," *Life*, May 5, 1967, 84–95; Warren Weaver Jr., "Romney Sounds an Uncertain Trumpet," *New York Times Magazine*, November 19, 1967.

31 Chris Bachelder, "Crashing the Party: The Ill-Fated 1968 Presidential Campaign of Governor George Romney," *Michigan Historical Review* 33, no. 2 (2007): 131–62.

32   Charles M. Lamb, *Housing Segregation in Suburban America Since 1960: Presidential and Judicial Politics* (Cambridge: Cambridge University Press, 2005), 85–93.

33   Robert Mason, *Richard Nixon and the Quest for a New Majority* (Raleigh: University of North Carolina Press, 2004), 149–50.

34   Lamb, *Housing Segregation,* 64–66.

35   Bart Barnes, "George W. Romney Dies at 88; Michigan Governor, HUD Secretary," *Washington Post,* July 27, 1995.

36   Niel Swidey and Stephanie Ebbert, "The Making of Mitt Romney: Journeys of a Shared Life: Raising Sons, Rising Expectations Bring Unexpected Turns," *Boston Globe,* June 27, 2007.

37   Frank Phillips, "Romney to Stump for Former In-law; His Father Backs Rival Mich. Hopeful," *Boston Globe,* July 26, 1994, 19.

38   David Rosenbaum, "George Romney Dies at 88: A Leading G.O.P. Figure," *The New York Times,* July 27, 1995.

39   Conger, "Evangelicals."

40   Burton Hersh, *The Shadow President: Ted Kennedy in Opposition* (Hanover, N.H.: Steelforth Press, 1997), 152–53.

41   Niel Swidey and Michael Paulson, "The Making of Mitt Romney," http://www.boston.com/news/politics/2008/specials/romney/part1/.

42   Swidey and Paulson, "The Making of Mitt Romney"; Michael Barone, and Grant Ujifusa, *The Almanac of American Politics* (Washington, D.C.: National Journal, 1999), 772; R. W. Apple Jr., "The 1994 Campaign: Massachusetts; Kennedy and Romney Meet, and the Rancor Flows Freely," *New York Times,* October 26, 1994, accessed July 10, 2010, http://www.nytimes.com/1994/10/26/us/1994-campaign-massachusetts-kennedy-romney-meet-rancor-flows-freely.html. When running for governor of Massachusetts, Romney's pro-choice position was viewed suspiciously by women's groups and Democrats. He would later reject that position when he ran for the presidency, but that only magnified charges of political opportunism.

43   Swidey and Paulson, "The Making of Mitt Romney."

44   Kirk Johnson, "In Olympic Success, Romney Found New Edge," *The New York Times,* September 19, 2007; also refer to Mitt Romney with Timothy Robinson, *Turnaround: Crisis, Leadership, and the Olympic Games* (Washington, D.C.: Regnery, 2004), 4.

45   Romney, *Turnaround,* 269.

46   Romney, *Turnaround,* 272, 276.

47   Romney, *Turnaround,* 281–82.

48   Romney, *Turnaround,* 278.

49   Barone and Cohen, *The Almanac of American Politics 2008,* 789.

50 Romney, *Turnaround*, xi–xii; "Mr. Smooth of Massachusetts," *Economist*, July 7, 2007.

51 Romney, *Turnaround*, xiv; Clive Crook, "The Massachusetts Experiment," *Atlantic,* June 27, 2006, http://www.theatlantic.com/magazine/archive/2006/06/the-massachusetts-experiment/5048/.

52 Rasmussen Reports, "Daily Presidential Tracking Poll History," http://www.rasmussenreports.com/public_content/politics/elections2/election_20082/daily_presidential_tracking_polling_history; "For GOP in Iowa, a Test whether Money Talks," *Boston Globe*, January 3, 2008.

53 "Electability Seen as Key to McCain's Rising Support," *Reuters*, February 1, 2008.

54 Liz Sidoti, "McCain Seals GOP Nod as Romney Drops Out," *Star Telegram*, February 7, 2008.

55 Michael Levenson, "Limbaugh's Praise for Romney Heard Loud and Clear," *Boston Globe*, January 18, 2008; "Coulter Wants Clinton over McCain," *CNN Political Ticker*, February 1, 2008, http://politicalticker.blogs.cnn.com/2008/02/01/coulter-wants-clinton-over-mccain/?fbid=MT5ALGn9Aex; Michael Luo, "Romney Embraces Theme Used to Beat Him," *The New York Times*, January 5, 2008.

56 "Transcript: Mass. Gov. Mitt Romney on 'FSN' Fox News Sunday with Chris Wallace," February 27, 2006, http://www.foxnews.com/story/0,2933,186080,00.html.

57 Zev Chaefts, "The Huckabee Factor," *New York Times Magazine*, December 12, 2007.

58 Quoted in Katharine Q. Seelye, "Apologies from the Heart of Darkness," *The New York Times*, December 14, 2007.

59 Lisa Lerer, "Romney Pays Tribute to Late Mormon Leader," *Politico*, January 28, 2008; "Republican Debate," *The New York Times*, January 24, 2008.

60 "Transcript: Mitt Romney's Faith Speech," *The New York Times*, December 6, 2007.

61 "Quotable: Romney's Religion Speech; Links to National Editorials, Columns," *Deseret News*, December 8, 2007; Conger, "Evangelicals."

62 Frank Phillips, "Romney Paves Way for Possible '12 Run," *Boston Globe*, December 8, 2008.

63 "Romney Picked as 2012 GOP Frontrunner," CNN Politics.com, http://www.cnn.com/2009/POLITICS/02/28/cpac/index.html; Kyle Trygstad, "Romney Wins SRLC Straw Poll," The Real Clear Politics, April 10, 2010, http://realclearpolitics.blogs.time.com/2010/04/10/romney-wins-srlc-straw-poll/; Ewen MacAskill, "Mitt Romney Beats Sarah Palin in Republican Straw Poll," *Guardian*, April 11, 2010.

64 "Romney Picked as 2012 GOP Frontrunner."

65 Florence Williams, "The Coyote Caucus Takes the West to Washington," *High Country News*, October 11, 2004, accessed April 1, 2010, http://www.hcn.org/issues/284/15040.

66 In backing Carter for the presidency, Mayor Young of Detroit said that Udall was not a viable candidate because of his affiliation with the LDS Church. "I'm askin' you to make a choice between a man from Georgia who fights to let you in his church, and a man from Arizona whose church won't even let you in the back door." Even though Udall had been endorsed by Representative John Conyers Jr., an African American from Detroit, Udall's message concerning his separation from the LDS Church "appear[ed] not to be getting across." Udall immediately asked for an apology from the mayor and for Carter to renounce these statements. The LDS Church prohibited otherwise worthy black men from holding the priesthood, a Mormon title of authority, until 1978.

67 Perhaps not surprisingly, Udall said, "If I am nominated, I will not carry Utah." J. Margolis, "Mo Udall Drops His 'Liberal' Tag," *Chicago Tribune*, March 31, 1976. He reinforced this attitude with a slight antireligious sentiment, saying, "I have no personal need for organized religious activity." R. Chandler, "'God Factor' Emerging in U.S. Politics," *Los Angeles Times*, May 30, 1976.

68 Rebecca Boyle, "Rep. Mark Udall Hopes to Extend His Family's Dynasty into the U.S. Senate," *Fort Collins Now*, May 30, 2008, accessed June 10, 2010, http://www.fortcollinsnow.com/article/20080530/NEWS/154286172. Mark Udall, like other members of his family, ran on an environmental platform.

69 David Alire Garcia, "Senator Tom Udall?" *New Mexico Independent*, May 23, 2008, accessed August 1, 2010, http://newmexicoindependent.com/1178/senator-tom-udall.

70 Reid has said, "I think some of the most unChristian-like letters, phone calls, contacts I've had were from members of the [LDS] church, saying some of the most mean things that are not in the realm of our church doctrine or certainly Christianity." Thomas Burr, "Harry Reid: A Mormon in the Middle," *Salt Lake Tribune*, October 26, 2009, accessed August 1, 2010, http://www.sltrib.com/lds/ci_13629152.

71 Tyson Snow, "Sen. Reid Explains Mormonism and Liberal Agenda," *Universe*, February 24, 2001, accessed August 15, 2010, http://newsnet.byu.edu/story.cfm/13779.

72 Snow, "Sen. Reid Explains."

73 Sheena McFarland, "Reid Tells BYU Crowd That Socially Responsible Dems Mirror Mormon Values," *Salt Lake Tribune*, October 9, 2007, accessed

August 15, 2010, http://web.archive.org/web/20071013011413/http://www.sltrib.com/ci_7128071.

74 Americans for Democratic Action, "ADA's 2008 Congressional Voting Record" (PDF), vol. 64, no. 1, http://www.adaction.org/media/votingrecords/2008.pdf,; American Conservative Union, "2007 Votes by State Delegation," http://www.acuratings.org/2007all.htm#NV.

75 "Transcript for December 5, 2004," NBC News, *Meet the Press*, December 5, 2004, http://www.msnbc.msn.com/id/6646457/. Reid's belief that "abortions should be legal only when the pregnancy resulted from incest, rape, or when the life of the woman is endangered" is precisely the same as the official stance of the LDS Church. "Senator Harry M. Reid (NV)," Project Vote Smart, http://www.votesmart.org/npat.php?can_id=53320#408. "Public Issues: Abortion," Newsroom: The Official Church Resource for News Media, Opinion Leaders, and the Public, http://newsroom.lds.org/ldsnewsroom/eng/public-issues/abortion.

76 The LDS Church makes its stand on the issue of same-sex marriage unequivocal, affirming that "marriage between a man and a woman is ordained of God." "The Family: A Proclamation to the World," LDS.org, http://www.lds.org/library/display/0,4945,161-1-11-1,FF.html.

77 "Senator Harry M. Reid (NV)," Project Vote Smart, http://www.votesmart.org/npat.php?can_id=53320#408.

78 Fifty-three percent of Mormons describe themselves as Republican, which is twice the percentage in the general population. Michelle Boorstein, "The Mormon Question: How Much Will Mitt Romney's Faith Have on the 2008 Election?" *Washington Post*, December 14, 2007, accessed July 10, 2010, http://www.washingtonpost.com/wp-dyn/content/article/2007/12/14/AR2007121401781.html.

79 "One reason I ran was to knock down the prejudicial wall that exists. . . . I wanted to make it easier for the next candidate of my faith," said Hatch. Terry Eastland, "In 2008, Will It Be Mormon in America?" *Weekly Standard*, June 6, 2005.

80 "Hatch Abandons Presidential Bid," CNN.com, January 26, 2000, http://cnn.com/2000/ALLPOLITICS/stories/01/26/hatch/index.html.

81 L. Wayne, "Senator Hatch Runs with Credentials Far Weightier than His Ratings," *The New York Times*, January 22, 2002.

82 L. Eaton, "Running Hard in the Back of the Pack," *The New York Times*, December 17, 1999.

83 "I can't do anything about bigots or bigotry but I can do a lot about people who are misinformed about my faith and about some people who don't believe we are Christian," he said. "I don't know how they can say that because the name of the church is the Church of Jesus Christ of Latter-day

Saints." "Hatch Abandons Presidential Bid: Utah Senator Endorses Bush," CNN, January 26, 2000, http://archives.cnn.com/2000/ALLPOLITICS/stories/01/26/hatch/index.html.

84   Wayne, "Senator Hatch Runs."

85   Melinda Liu, "Mr. Huntsman Goes to Beijing," Newsweek, November 16, 2009, accessed August 15, 2010, http://www.newsweek.com/id/223058.

86   Kathleen Parker, "Health Reform, Utah's Way," Washington Post, July 24, 2009, accessed August 1, 2010, http://www.washingtonpost.com/wp-dyn/content/article/2009/07/24/AR2009072401956.html?sid=ST2009072802120.

87   In 2009, 70 percent of Utahans opposed civil unions. Mark Ambinder, "2012 and Huntsman's Surprise," Atlantic, February 13, 2009, accessed June 10, 2010, http://www.theatlantic.com/politics/archive/2009/02/2012-and-huntsmans-surprise/602/.

88   Lisa Riley Roche, "Huntsman Calls Self 'Moderating Voice' on Many Issues," Deseret News, February 10, 2009, accessed August 5, 2010, http://www.deseretnews.com/article/1,5143,705284093,00.html.

89   Accepting this position, Huntsman resigned from his post as governor of Utah.

90   Liu, "Mr. Huntsman Goes to Beijing."

91   "Election 2008: 43% Would Never Vote for Mormon Candidate," Rasmussen Reports, November 20, 2006. Comparatively, a Mormon would still fare better than an atheist; 54 percent of Americans would not vote for a person who did not believe in God. During the same years, only 4 percent of Americans were unwilling to vote for a Catholic, and 5 percent would not vote for a Jew. This means that Americans are over six times more likely to not vote for a Mormon candidate than they are to be similarly biased against a Catholic. "Percentage Unwilling to Vote for a Mormon Holds Steady," Gallup, December 11, 2007; "Questions and Answers about America's Religion," Gallup, December 24, 2007.

92   John Lillpop, "Anti-Mormon Bigotry Tainting Republican Votes?" Canada Free Press, February 5, 2008, accessed April 15, 2010, http://www.canadafreepress.com/index.php/article/1734.

93   Amy Sullivan, "Mitt Romney's Evangelical Problem," Washington Monthly, September 2005, accessed August 15, 2010, http://www.washingtonmonthly.com/features/2005/0509.sullivan1.html.

94   Christopher Orlet, "No Mormons Need Apply," American Spectator, February 14, 2008, accessed September 1, 2010, http://spectator.org/archives/2008/02/14/no-mormons-need-apply.

95   Mike Allen, "A Mormon as President?" Time, November 26, 2006,

accessed June 10, 2010, http://www.time.com/time/magazine/article/0,9171,1562941,00.html#ixzz0kT26JHpf.

96 Alex Beam, "Are We Ready for a Mormon President?" *Boston Globe*, July 21, 2005, accessed July 15, 2010, http://www.boston.com/news/globe/living/articles/2005/07/21/are_we_ready_for_a_mormon_president/.

7 Ezra Taft Benson, *The Constitution: A Heavenly Banner* (Salt Lake City: Deseret Book, 2008).

98 *Doctrine and Covenants* 101:80.

99 Upholding the freedoms America treasures is a job Church members take seriously. John Taylor, the third president of the Church, stated that it would one day be up to the Mormons to save the Constitution and the nation. "When the people shall have torn to shreds the Constitution of the United States," he said, "the Elders of Israel will be found holding it up to the nations of the earth, and proclaiming liberty and equal rights to all men, and extending the hand of fellowship to the oppressed of all nations." Taylor, *The Gospel Kingdom (Salt Lake City:* Deseret Book, 1943), 219. Also early in the history of the Church, another member of the LDS hierarchy, George Q. Cannon, said, "the day will come when the Constitution and free government under it will be sustained and preserved by this people." Tom L. Perry, "God's Hand in the Founding of America," *New Era*, July 1976, 45.

100 Hugh Hewitt, *Mormon in the White House? Ten Things Every American Should Know about Mitt Romney* (Washington, D.C.: Regnery, 2007), 221–31.

101 Hewitt, *Mormon in the White House?* 232.

Chapter 4

1 Eldon J. Eisenach, "Conclusion: Religion, Politics, and American Identity after September 11: Reflections on Recent Scholarship," in *Religion, Politics, and American Identity*, ed. David S. Gutterman and Andrew R. Murphy (Lanham, Md.: Lexington Books, 2006), 269–91.

2 The "burned-over district" is an area of central western New York State that saw particularly enthusiastic religious activity during the Second Great Awakening. Cross, *The Burned-over District.*

3 Joseph Smith, *History of the Church of Jesus Christ of Latter-day Saints*, 7 vols. (Salt Lake City: Deseret Book, 1978).

4 The story of Joseph Smith's vision of God and Jesus Christ is recorded in LDS scripture in a book called *Joseph Smith—History* 1:10.

5 *Joseph Smith—History* 1:12. Smith quotes from James 1:5 (KJV).

6 *Joseph Smith—History* 1:14-15.

7 *Joseph Smith—History* 1:19.

8   *Joseph Smith—History* 1:17.
9   Church Educational System, *Church History in the Fullness of Times Student Manual* (Salt Lake City: Church of Jesus Christ of Latter-day Saints, 2003).
10 Church Educational System, *Church History*.
11 Robert Remini, *Joseph Smith* (New York: Viking, 2002).
12 *Joseph Smith—History* 1:3.
13 LDS members, many of whom were already poor, often lost all of their property as they were encouraged to participate in the LDS policy of communitarianism, or the United Order.
14 Although the LDS suffered the brunt of this maltreatment, they were in some cases instigators of violence themselves. Such retaliations only served to increase animosity toward them.
15 *Another Testament of Jesus Christ* is the subtitle of the Book of Mormon.
16 Church Educational System, *Church History*.
17 Book of Mormon, introduction. Some have argued that the Book of Mormon (named after the ancient prophet who edited the writings around 500 A.D.), is an eighteenth-century document, written by Smith (rather than translated from an ancient text, as he claims). Brodie, *No Man Knows My History*. However, Smith and his followers saw it as "another testament of Christ," meant to complement the Old and New Testaments and believe that it was written by ancient prophets who foresaw the latter-days. Members of the LDS Church consider it to be the foundational text of their religion and are encouraged to read from the Book of Mormon daily. Many reason that if the Book of Mormon is true, then Smith was a divinely inspired prophet, and therefore the entire gospel as laid out by him is also correct. In this way, it acts as a kind of litmus test for the rest of Mormonism.
18 At this point, widespread war and mass killing led to the disintegration of society. The Book of Mormon also briefly tells the story of another people, the Jaredites, who came to America after the world's languages were confused at the Tower of Babel. The Nephite and Jaredite civilizations overlapped for a short time, though neither one discovered the other until there was only one Jaredite left. The Mulekites also traveled from Jerusalem to America shortly after the Nephites did, and later the two groups met and merged into one single civilization. Those who chose not to follow God's commandments were called Lamanites. The Hebraic origin of these civilizations makes them God's chosen people, just as Smith and his followers claimed to be. They were saved from being led captive into Babylon and led to a "promised land." Speaking of North America, the book says, "this is a land which is choice above all other lands; wherefore he that doth possess it shall serve God or shall be swept off; for it is the

everlasting decree of God. And it is not until the fulness of iniquity among the children of the land, that they are swept off" (Ether 2:10).

19 James E. Talmage, *Jesus the Christ* (Salt Lake City: Deseret Book, 1982).

20 Harold Bloom, *The American Religion* (New York: Chu Hartley Press, 2006); Richard L. Bushman, *Mormonism: A Very Short Introduction* (New York: Oxford University Press, 2008).

21 Bloom, *The American Religion*; Bushman, *Mormonism*.

22 Bloom, *The American Religion*, 113.

23 Speaking of man's eternal destiny, Smith said, "God was once as we are now, and is an exalted man, and sits enthroned in yonder heavens! That is the great secret. . . . I might with boldness proclaim from the housetops that God never had the power to create the spirit of man at all. God himself could not create himself." Joseph Smith, *Teachings of the Prophet Joseph Smith*, ed. Joseph F. Smith Jr. (Salt Lake City: Deseret News Press, 1965), 342–45.

24 When speaking of the future salvation of man, Smith said of the state of those who were most righteous after the resurrection, "Then shall they be gods, because they have no end; therefore shall they be from everlasting to everlasting, because they continue; then shall they be above all, because all things are subject unto them. Then shall they be gods, because they have all power, and the angels are subject unto them." *Doctrine and Covenants* 132:20. This was the case with Abraham, Isaac, and Jacob, Smith went on to explain, because they had kept the commandments, and so "they sit upon thrones, and are not angels, but are gods." *Doctrine and Covenants* 132:21.

25 Church Educational System, *Church History*; Winder, *Presidents and Prophets*.

26 This is why the LDS Church is highly involved in family history research.

27 Pew Research Center, "A Post-Election Look at Religious Voters in the 2008 Elections," Pew Research Forum, December 8, 2008, accessed April 1, 2010, http://pewforum.org/Politics-and-Elections/A-Post-Election-Look -at-Religious-Voters-in-the-2008-Election.aspx.

28 The general population refers to all Americans regardless of their religious beliefs. Pew Research Center, "A Portrait of Mormons in the U.S.," Pew Research Forum, July 24, 2009, accessed April 1, 2010, http://pewforum .org/Christian/Mormon/A-Portrait-of-Mormons-in-the-US-Social-and -Political-Views.aspx.

29 Interestingly, only 9 percent of Mormons oppose abortion in all cases, whereas 61 percent oppose it in most cases. In contrast, 25 percent of evangelicals oppose abortion in all cases and 36 percent in most cases. Pew Research Center, "A Portrait of Mormons in the U.S."

30 Pew Research Center, "A Portrait of Mormons in the U.S." Also refer to Wayne K. Hinton and Stephen Roberds, "Public Opinion, Culture, and Religion in Utah," in *Utah in the Twentieth Century*, edited by Brian Q.

Cannon and Jessie L. Embry (Logan: Utah State University Press, 2009), 227–44.

31 Pew Research Center, "A Portrait of Mormons in the U.S."

32 Pew Research Center, "A Portrait of Mormons in the U.S."

33 Pew Research Center, "Public Opinion about Mormons," Pew Research Forum, December 4, 2007, accessed April 1, 2010, http://pewresearch .org/pubs/648/romney-mormon.

34 Pew Research Center, "Public Opinion about Mormons."

35 Pew Research Center, "Public Opinion about Mormons."

36 Pew Research Center, "Public Opinion about Mormons."

37 Gerald R. McDermott, "How Do We Know about Jesus?" in *Claiming Christ*, ed. Robert L. Millet and Gerald R. McDermott (Grand Rapids: Brazos Press, 2007), 15–29; Craig L. Blomberg and Stephen E. Robinson, *How Wide the Divide? A Mormon and an Evangelical in Conversation* (Downers Grove, Ill.: InterVarsity Press, 1997).

38 McDermott, "How Do We Know about Jesus?" 16.

39 McDermott, "How Do We Know about Jesus?" 16–18. Also refer to N. T. Wright, *What Saint Paul Really Said* (Grand Rapids: Eerdmans, 1997).

40 It may appear to some that the debate about the creedal or non-creedal character of religion is trivial; however, to some Christians and Mormons, this is a point of contention and division among them. In interpreting the Bible, some Christians rely upon the traditional creeds as grounded in a systematic metaphysics derived from Greek philosophical categories, while other Christian denominations reject them. By contrast, Mormons use creeds in their interpretation of the Bible and Book of Mormon, but these creeds are not rooted in classical Greek philosophy.

41 Robert L. Millet, *A Different Jesus? The Christ of Latter-day Saints* (Grand Rapids: Eerdmans, 2005), 55.

42 The Articles of Faith are an authoritative statement written by Smith that clarifies the LDS position on several issues and sets out some of the key tenets of the faith. Among other things, the Articles state the LDS belief in God the Father, Jesus Christ, and the Holy Ghost, the Atonement, which saves mankind from sin, the principles of faith, repentance, and baptism, a belief in past and continuing revelation, and the importance of honesty, virtue, chastity, and "doing good to all men." Interestingly, and likely in response to the persecutions the Church was facing at the time, the Articles also include the following statement of tolerance: "We claim the privilege of worshiping Almighty God according to the dictates of our own conscience and allow all men the same privilege, let them worship how, where, or what they may" (11).

43 Blomberg and Robinson, *How Wide the Divide?*, 55. According to BYU

historian Grant Underwood, Mormons have given Joseph Smith the same canonical status as the apostle Paul. Grant Underwood, "Mormons and the Millennial World-View," in *Mormon Identities in Transition*, ed. Douglas J. Davies (New York: Cassell, 1996), 141. For more debate about the Mormon canon, refer to W. D. Davies, "Reflections on the Mormon Canon," *Harvard Theological Review* 79, no. 1 (1986): 44–66.

44 Jan Shipps, *Sojourner in the Promised Land: Forty Years among the Mormons* (Urbana: University of Illinois Press, 2000), 31; Shipps, "Is Mormonism Christian? Reflections on a Complicated Question," in *Mormons and Mormonism: An Introduction to an American World Religion*, ed. Eric A. Eliason (Urbana: University of Illinois Press, 2001), 83.

45 Philip Barlow, *Mormonism and the Bible: The Place of Latter-day Saints in American Religion* (New York: Oxford University Press, 1991), 220.

46 Givens claim that Mormonism provides a new type of ongoing revelation, dialogic, that differs from traditional accounts of divine revelation (for example, doctrine, history, or experience). This new revelation not only differs in its form of communication but also in its nature as a continuous, ongoing process. Terryl L. Givens, "The Book of Mormon and Religious Epistemology," *Dialogue* 34, nos. 3–4 (2001): 31–54, especially 39–40; *By the Hand of Mormon: The American Scripture that Launched a New World Religion* (Oxford: Oxford University Press, 2002).

47 Millet, *A Different Jesus*, 78, 16.

48 Millet, *A Different Jesus*, 26.

49 Blomberg and Robinson, *How Wide the Divide?*, 57.

50 Blomberg and Robinson, *How Wide the Divide?*, 64.

51 Blomberg and Robinson, *How Wide the Divide?*, 36, 63; Richard John Neuhaus, "Is Mormonism Christian?" *First Things* (March 2000): 97–115.

52 Bruce D. Porter and Gerald D. McDermott, "Is Mormonism Christian?" *First Things* (October 2008).

53 Mormons would respond to McDermott's critique that the Jesus of the LDS Church is also the Jesus of the four gospels. Mormons also accept the Bible as divine revelation, as mainstream Christians. However, they also claim the Book of Mormon is not a modern scripture but is an ancient one that was recently translated. Givens, *By the Hand of Mormon*; Grant Hardy, *Understanding the Book of Mormon: A Reader's Guide* (Oxford: Oxford University Press, 2010).

54 Neuhaus, "Is Mormonism Christian?"

55 Peggy Fletcher Stack, "Muslim Clerics: We Can Learn from the Mormons," *Salt Lake Tribune*, February 11, 2010. Also refer to Maqbool Ahmed, "A Muslim Family in Utah," in *God and Country: Politics in Utah*, ed. Jeffery E. Sells. (Salt Lake City: Signature Books, 2005), 325–40. For more

about the acceptance of Muslims in the United States, refer to James M. Penning, "Americans' Views of Muslims and Mormons: A Social Identity Theory of Approach," *Religion and Politics* 2 (2009): 277–302.

56   Frederick L. Wegner, "Living a Jewish Life in Utah Society," in Sells, *God and Country*, 319–24; Raphael Jospe, Truman G. Madsen, and Seth Ward, eds., *Covenant and Chosenness in Judaism and Mormonism* (Madison: Fairleigh Dickinson University Press, 2001); Frank Johnson and William J. Leffler. *Jews and Mormons: Two Houses of Israel* (Hoboken, N.J.: Ktav, 2000).

57   Technically (so they claim) Mormons are part of the House of Joseph, which can trace its lineage to these original tribes.

58   Bernard I. Kouchel, "A Chronicle of the Mormon Baptism of Jewish Holocaust Victims," JewishGen, http://www.jewishgen.org/infofiles/ldsagree.html.

59   Kouchel, "A Chronicle."

60   Kouchel, "A Chronicle."

Chapter 5

1   Alexis de Tocqueville, *Democracy in America* (Chicago: University of Chicago Press, 2002), 280.

2   Tocqueville, *Democracy in America.*

3   Tocqueville, *Democracy in America*, 282.

4   Tocqueville, *Democracy in America*, 275, 278.

5   Richard Ostling and Joan Ostling, *Mormon America: The Power and Promise* (San Francisco: HarperOne, 1999), xvi, xix.

6   Antonio Reyes, "Mormonism, Americanism, and Mexico," *American Behavioral Scientist* 40, no. 7 (1997): 902–13.

7   Terryl L. Givens, *The Latter-day Saint Experience in America* (Westport, Conn.: Greenwood Press, 2004).

8   Bloom, *The American Religion*; Thomas Yates, "Count Tolstoi and 'The American Religion,'" *Improvement Era* 42 (1939): 32.

9   "Count Leo Tolstoy, Russian author and statesman, in conversation with Andrew D. White, United States Foreign Minister to Russia, in 1892 said,

'I wish you would tell me about your American religion.'

" 'We have no state church in America,' replied Dr. White.

" 'I know that, but what about your American religion?'

"Dr. White explained to Tolstoy that in America each person is free to belong to the particular church in which he is interested.

"Tolstoy impatiently replied: 'I know all of this, but I want to know about the *American* religion. . . . The church to which I refer originated in America and is commonly known as the Mormon Church. What can you tell me of the teachings of the Mormons?'

"Dr. White said, 'I know very little concerning them.'

"Then Count Leo Tolstoy rebuked the ambassador. 'Dr. White, I am greatly surprised and disappointed that a man of your great learning and position should be so ignorant on this important subject. Their principles teach the people not only of heaven and its attendant glories, but how to live so that their social and economic relations with each other are placed on a sound basis. If the people follow the teachings of this church, nothing can stop their progress—it will be limitless.'

"Tolstoy continued, 'There have been great movements started in the past but they have died or been modified before they reached maturity. If Mormonism is able to endure, unmodified, until it reaches the third and fourth generation, it is destined to become the greatest power the world has ever known.' " (David Haight, "He Is Not Here, He Is Risen," *Ensign*, May 1980, 9. This conversation is also cited in Bloom, *The American Religion*, 116, emphasis in the original.)

According to one historian, "The central concern of the Jacksonian generation was the transition from a society based on tradition [strict morality and religious piety] to a society based on an ethic of individualism." Lawrence Kohol, *The Politics of Individualism: Parties and the American Character in the Jacksonian Era* (Oxford: Oxford University Press, 1989), 6.

10   Bloom, *The American Religion*, 129.

11   Homer Durham, "A Political Interpretation of Mormon History," *Pacific Historical Review* 13, no. 2 (1994): 136.

12   Maxine Hanks and Jean Kinney Williams, *Mormon Faith in America* (New York: Facts on File, 2003), 25, 51.

13   Daniel Walker Howe, *What Hath God Wrought: The Transformation of America, 1815–1848* (Oxford: Oxford University Press, 2007).

14   Kohol, *The Politics of Individualism*.

15   Harry L. Watson, *Liberty and Power: The Politics of Jacksonian America* (New York: Hill & Wang, 2006).

16   Craig James Hazen, *The Village Enlightenment in America: Popular Religion and Science in the Nineteenth Century* (Urbana: University of Illinois Press, 2000), 21; White, "Mormonism in America and Canada."

17   Klaus J. Hansen, "Joseph Smith and the Political Kingdom of God," *American West* 5 (1968): 21.

18   These are words taken from an LDS pioneer hymn, "Come, Come, Ye Saints," which commemorates the pioneer trek. The third verse says, "We'll find a place which God for us prepared, / Far away, in the West, / Where none shall come to hurt or make afraid; / There the Saints will be blessed." William Clayton, "Come, Come, Ye Saints," *Hymns of the Church of Jesus Christ of Latter-day Saints* (Salt Lake City: Church of Jesus Christ of Latter-day Saints), 30.

19   Walter Nugent, *Habits of Empire: A History of American Expansion* (New York: Alfred A. Knopf, 2008).

20   Jessie L. Embry, *Mormon Polygamous Families: Life in the Principle* (Draper, Utah: Greg Kofford Books, 2006).

21   White, "Mormonism in America and Canada," 163.

22   Bloom, *The American Religion*, 70.

23   Robert Gottlieb and Peter Wiley, *America's Saints: The Rise of Mormon Power* (New York: Putnam, 1984), 37.

24   Similarities between Smith's cultural experience and the religion he founded are also sources for criticism of Mormonism. White argues that "*The Book of Mormon* clearly reflects the major preoccupations of nineteenth century Americans" ("Mormonism in America and Canada," 162). Howe expresses a similar perspective, although he adds that "the dominant themes" of the Book of Mormon "are biblical, prophetic, and patriarchal, not democratic or optimistic" (*What Hath God Wrought*, 314). Members of the LDS Church today often counter such arguments against the Book of Mormon's authenticity by saying that any correlations between the book and nineteenth-century America are evidence that God prepared the book specifically for Smith's generation (and those that would follow).

25   "Latter-day Saints know, through modern revelation, that the Garden of Eden was on the North American continent and that Adam and Eve began their conquest of the earth in the upper part of what is now the state of Missouri. It seems very probable that the children of our first earthly parents moved down along the fertile, pleasant lands of the Mississippi valley." John A. Widstoe, *Evidences and Reconciliations* (Salt Lake City: Bookcraft, 1960), 127.

26   This repositioning of the Holy Land in the New World also meant that the LDS cast themselves as the chosen people—often buffeted and persecuted, but always blessed, and they prospered by the hand of God. Bloom, *The American Religion*. Also refer to Christian Gellinek and Richard Hacken, "Christ in America? Mormonism as a Christian Religion in Comparative Ecclesiastical History," *Brigham Young University Studies* 39, no. 1 (2000): 212–15.

27   Ezra Taft Benson, *The Constitution: A Heavenly Banner* (Salt Lake City: Deseret Book, 2008).

28   Stephen J. Fleming, "Congenial to Almost Every Shade of Radicalism: The Delaware Valley and the Success of Early Mormonism," *Religion and American Culture* 17, no. 2 (2007): 129–64; Joseph Smith, *History of the Church of Jesus Christ of Latter-day Saints*, 7 vols. (Salt Lake City: Deseret Book, 1978).

29   Nathan O. Hatch, "The Populist View of Joseph Smith," in *Mormons and Mormonism*, ed. E. A. Eliason (Urbana: University of Illinois Press, 2001),

123–36; M. Pillis, "The Social Sources of Mormonism," in *American Church History: A Reader,* ed. H. Warner (Nashville: Abingdon, 1998), 346–56.

30 This is only one of many instances of how the LDS re-enact the history of the Hebraic religious tradition. According to Bloom, "near identification with the ancient Hebrews" was typical of Americans of Smith's generation who "had drowned in the Bible." Bloom, *The American Religion,* 78.

31 For more about the Mormon westward migration, refer to Leonard J. Arrington and Davis Bitton, *The Mormon Experience: A History of the Latter-day Saints* (New York: Knopf, 1979), 44–82.

32 Arrington and Bitton, *The Mormon Experience,* 101–5, 127–44.

33 Ethan R. Yorgason, *Transformation of the Mormon Culture Region* (Urbana: University of Illinois Press, 2003).

34 Fred E. Woods, *A Gamble in the Desert: The Mission in Las Vegas (1855–57)* (Salt Lake City: Mormon Historic Sites Foundation, 2005).

35 *Resolution Urging Jell-O Recognition,* 2001 General Session, State of Utah, sponsored by the Honorable Leonard M. Blackham, accessed April 15, 2010, http://www.le.state.ut.us/~2001/bills/sbillenr/SR0005.htm.

36 Yorgason, *Transformation of the Mormon Culture Region.*

37 "Deseret" is derived from the word for "honeybee" in the Book of Mormon.

38 Matt 6:10 (KJV). Marvin S. Hill, *Quest for Refuge: The Flight from American Pluralism* (Salt Lake City: Signature Books, 1989), 56.

39 Refer to the Mormon *Doctrine and Covenants* 98:5-6: "And that law of the land which is constitutional, supporting that principle of freedom in maintaining rights and privileges, belongs to all mankind, and is justifiable before me. Therefore, I, the Lord, justify you, and your brethren of my church, in befriending that law which is the constitutional law of the land." Also refer to Michael D. Quinn, "The Council of Fifty and Its Members, 1844–1945," *BYU Studies* 20, no. 2 (1980): 163–98; and Andrew F. Ehat, "It Seems Like Heaven Began on Earth: Joseph Smith and the Constitution of the Kingdom of God," *BYU Studies* 20, no. 3 (1980): 253–79.

40 Quinn, "The Council of Fifty."

41 Edwin Brown Firmage and Richard Collin Mangrum, *Zion in the Courts: A Legal History of the Church of Jesus Christ of Latter-day Saints, 1830–1900* (Champaign: University of Illinois Press 1988), 11.

42 Ehat, "It Seems Like Heaven."

43 James T. McHugh, "A Liberal Theocracy: Philosophy, Theology, and Utah Constitutional Law," *Albany Law Review* 60 (1996–97): 1515, 1520.

44 Ehat, "It Seems Like Heaven."

45 Glenn M. Leonard, "The Mormon Boundary Question in the 1849–50 Statehood Debates," *Journal of Mormon History* 18, no. 1 (1992): 114–36; Peter Crawley, "The Constitution of the State of Deseret," *BYU Studies* 29, no. 4 (1989): 7.

46 Leonard, "The Mormon Boundary Question"; Crawley, "The Constitution."

47 Nevertheless, President Taylor sent his representative, John Wilson, westward with a proposal to combine California and Deseret into a single state. The result would have been to decrease the number of free states entering the Union, thus preserving the balance of power between free states and slave states in the Senate. Leonard, "The Mormon Boundary Question"; Crawley, "The Constitution"; Arrington and Bitton, *The Mormon Experience*, 163–65.

48 Leonard, "The Mormon Boundary Question"; Crawley, "The Constitution."

49 Leonard, "The Mormon Boundary Question"; Crawley, "The Constitution."

50 James B. Allen and Glen M. Leonard, *The Story of the Latter-day Saints* (Salt Lake City: Deseret Books, 1976).

51 Arrington and Bitton, *The Mormon Experience*, 164; also refer to Sarah Barringer Gordon, *The Mormon Question: Polygamy and Constitutional Conflict in Nineteenth Century America* (Chapel Hill: University of North Carolina Press, 2002).

52 Arrington and Bitton, *The Mormon Experience*, 164–72; also refer to Norman F. Furniss, *The Utah Conflict: 1850–1859* (New Haven: Yale University Press, 2005).

53 Furniss, *The Utah Conflict*.

54 Allen and Leonard, *The Story of the Latter-day Saints*, 298–99.

55 William P. MacKinnon, "Loose in the Stacks: A Half-Century with the Utah War and Its Legacy," *Dialogue* 40, no. 1 (2007): 43–81.

56 Furniss, *The Utah Conflict*.

57 Furniss, *The Utah Conflict*.

58 Richard Douglas Poll, *The Quixotic Mediator: Thomas L. Kane and the Utah War* (Ogden, Utah: Weber State College Press, 1985).

59 Allen and Leonard, *The Story of the Latter-day Saints*, 308.

60 Leroy R. Hafen and Ann W. Hafen, eds., *Mormon Resistance: A Documentary Account of the Utah Expedition, 1857–1858* (Lincoln: University of Nebraska Press, 2005), 39–40.

61 There are several accounts of the Mountain Meadow massacre. The most objective one is Juanita Brooks, *The Mountain Meadow Massacre* (Norman: University of Oklahoma Press, 2003).

62 Arrington and Bitton, *The Mormon Experience*, 164–84.

63 However, President Lincoln did not enforce the Act, in exchange for Brigham Young not becoming involved in the Civil War. Nevertheless, Judge Kinney issued a writ against Young for violation of the Act, but an all-Mormon grand jury refused to indict him, citing lack of evidence of Young's marriage to Amelia Folsom. Firmage and Mangrum, *Zion in the Courts*, 139; also see Furniss, *The Mormon Conflict*, 63.

64 Reed Smoot was an LDS church leader who was elected to the US Senate in 1903. His fellow congressmen did not want to seat him, however, because they felt that as a leader in the LDS Church, he was responsible for the covert continuation of polygamy which had been reported, and that his loyalty to the U.S. Constitution was in question. The trials lasted from 1904–1907, and though Smoot was allowed to participate in congress during this time, but the Senate ultimately voted to exclude him.

65 Armand Mauss argues that by the mid-twentieth century the LDS ideal of family life was no different than that of other Americans. Mauss, *The Angel and the Beehive*.

66 E. L. Thorndike, "The Origins of Superior Men," *Scientific Monthly*, May 1943, 424–32; Kenneth R. Hardy, "Social Origins of American Scientists and Scholars," *Science*, August 9, 1974, 497–506.

67 Mauss, *The Angel and the Beehive*, 28.

68 At the end of 2009, Church membership had reached over 13.8 million worldwide. In the United States, less than 2 percent of the total adult population describe themselves as LDS, making the Church the tenth most common denomination in the country. Pew Research Forum, "A Portrait of Mormons in the US," Pew Forum on Religion and Public Life, July 24, 2009, http://pewforum.org/Christian/Mormon/A-Portrait-of-Mormons -in-the-US.aspx.

79 Antonio Reyes, "Mormonism, Americanism, and Mexico," *American Behavioral Scientist* 40, no. 7 (1997): 902–13.

70 John F. Kennedy, "Address at the Mormon Tabernacle (September 26, 1963)," Miller Center of Public Affairs, accessed August 1, 2010, http:// millercenter.org/scripps/archive/speeches/detail/3378 (emphasis added).

SELECTED BIBLIOGRAPHY

Ahmed, Maqbool. "A Muslim Family in Utah." In *God and Country: Politics in Utah*, edited by Jeffery E. Sells, 325–40. Salt Lake City: Signature Books, 2005.

Allen, James B., and Glen M. Leonard. *The Story of the Latter-day Saints*. Salt Lake City: Deseret Books, 1976.

Allen, Mike. "A Mormon as President?" *Time*, November 26, 2006. Accessed June 10, 2010. http://www.time.com/time/magazine/article/0,9171,1562941,00.html#ixzz0kT26JHpf.

Allen, Mike, and Carrie Budoff Brown. "Huntsman Chosen China Ambassador." CBS News Politico, May 15, 2009. Accessed June 10, 2010. http://www.cbsnews.com/stories/2009/05/16/politics/politico/main5019678.shtml.

Alley, Robert. *The Constitution and Religion: Leading Supreme Court Cases on Church and State*. Amherst, N.Y.: Prometheus Books, 1999.

Altman, Irwin, and Joseph Grant. *Polygamous Families in Contemporary Societies*. Cambridge: Cambridge University Press, 1996.

Ambinder, Mark. "2012 and Huntsman's Surprise." *Atlantic*, February 13, 2009. Accessed June 10, 2010. http://www.theatlantic.com/politics/archive/2009/02/2012-and-huntsmans-surprise/602/.

Apple, R. W., Jr. "The 1994 Campaign: Massachusetts; Kennedy and Romney Meet, and the Rancor Flows Freely." *New York Times*, October 26, 1994. Accessed July 10, 2010. http://www.nytimes.com/1994/10/26/us/1994-campaign-massachusetts-kennedy-romney-meet-rancor-flows-freely.html.

Arrington, Leonard J. *Great Basin Kingdom: An Economic History of the Latter-day Saints, 1830–1900.* 3rd ed. Urbana: University of Illinois Press, 2004.

Arrington, Leonard J., and Davis Bitton. *The Mormon Experience: A History of the Latter-day Saints.* New York: Knopf, 1979.

Atkinson, Sally. "America's Next Top Mormon: Reality-TV Shows Are Plucking Contestants from an Unlikely Pew." *Newsweek*, May 19, 2008. Accessed April 1, 2010. http://www.newsweek.com/id/136340.

Bachelder, Chris. "Crashing the Party: The Ill-Fated 1968 Presidential Campaign of Governor George Romney." *Michigan Historical Review* 33, no. 2 (2007): 131–62.

Baer, Hans A. *Recreating Utopia in the Desert: A Sectarian Challenge to Modern Mormonism.* Albany: State University of New York Press, 1988.

Barlow, Philip. *Mormonism and the Bible: The Place of Latter-day Saints in American Religion.* New York: Oxford University Press, 1991.

Barone, Michael, and Richard E. Cohen. *The Almanac of American Politics, 2008.* Washington, D.C.: National Journal, 2008.

Barone, Michael, and Grant Ujifusa. *The Almanac of American Politics.* Washington D.C.: National Journal, 1999.

Beam, Alex. "Are We Ready for a Mormon President?" *Boston Globe*, July 21, 2005. Accessed July 15, 2010. http://www.boston.com/news/globe/living/articles/2005/07/21/are_we_ready_for_a_mormon_president/.

Beck, Glenn. *Arguing with Idiots: How to Stop Small Minds and Big Government.* New York: Threshold Editions, 2009.

————. *The Christmas Sweater.* New York: Threshold Editions, 2008.

————. *Glenn Beck's Common Sense: The Case Against Out-of-Control Government, Inspired by Thomas Paine.* New York: Threshold Editions, 2009.

————. "Glenn Beck Story Pulled Because of His Mormon Faith."

The Glenn Beck Program, January 4, 2009. Accessed April 1, 2010. http://www.glennbeck.com/content/articles/article/200/19594.

————. *An Inconvenient Book: Real Solutions to the World's Biggest Problems*. New York: Threshold Editions, 2007.

————. *The Real America: Messages from the Heart and Heartland*. New York: Simon and Schuster, 2005.

Benson, Ezra Taft. *The Constitution: A Heavenly Banner*. Salt Lake City: Deseret Book, 2008.

Bigler, D. L. *Forgotten Kingdom: The Mormon Theocracy in the American West, 1847–1896*. Logan: Utah State University Press, 1998.

Blomberg, Craig L., and Stephen E. Robinson. *How Wide the Divide? A Mormon and an Evangelical in Conversation*. Downers Grove, Ill.: InterVarsity Press, 1997.

Bloom, Harold. *The American Religion*. New York: Chu Hartley Press, 2006.

Boorstein, Michelle. "The Mormon Question: How Much Impact Will Mitt Romney's Faith Have on the 2008 Election?" *Washington Post*, December 14, 2007. Accessed July 10, 2010. http://www.washingtonpost.com/wp-dyn/content/article/2007/12/14/AR2007121401781.html.

Boyle, Rebecca. "Rep. Mark Udall Hopes to Extend His Family's Dynasty into the U.S. Senate." *Fort Collins Now*, May 30, 2008. Accessed June 10, 2010. http://www.fortcollinsnow.com/article/20080530/NEWS/154286172.

Brace, Paul. *State Government and Economic Performance*. Baltimore: Johns Hopkins University Press, 1994.

Bradlee, Ben, Jr. and Dale Van Atta. *Prophet of Blood: The Untold Story of Ervil LeBaron and the Lambs of God*. New York: Putnam, 1981.

Bradley, Martha Sonntag. *Kidnapped from That Land: The Government Raids on the Short Creek Polygamists*. Salt Lake City: University of Utah Press, 1993.

Brodie, Fawn M. *No Man Knows My History: The Life of Joseph Smith*. New York: Vintage, 1995.

Brooks, Joanna. "How Mormonism Built Glenn Beck." *Religious Dispatches*, October 27, 2009. Accessed April 1, 2010. http://

www.religiondispatches.org/archive/religiousright/1885/
how_mormonism_built_glenn_beck?page=entire.

Brooks, Juanita. *The Mountain Meadow Massacre*. Norman: University of Oklahoma Press, 2003.

Burgess, Steve. "Donny Osmond: We Suffer for His Art." Salon.com, September 21, 1999. Accessed April 1, 2010. http://www.salon.com/people/feature/1999/09/21/osmond/index.html.

Burr, Thomas. "Harry Reid: A Mormon in the Middle." *Salt Lake Tribune*, October 26, 2009. Accessed August 1, 2010. http://www.sltrib.com/lds/ci_13629152.

Bushman, Richard L. *Joseph Smith and the Beginnings of Mormonism*. Urbana: University of Illinois Press, 1984.

————. *Joseph Smith: A Rough Stone Rolling*. New York: Vintage, 2007.

————. *Mormonism: A Very Short Introduction*. New York: Oxford University Press, 2008.

Bushman, Richard L., and Claudia Lauper Bushman. *Mormons in America*. Oxford: Oxford University Press, 1999.

Bushman, Richard L., and Damon Linker, "Mitt Romney's Mormonism: A TNR Debate." *New Republic*, January 3–5, 2007. Accessed August 1, 2010. http://www.tnr.com/article/politics/mitt-romneys-mormonism.

Campbell, Joel. "Focus on Family Pulls Glenn Beck Article." *Mormon Times*, December 27, 2008. Accessed April 1, 2010. http://www.mormontimes.com/mormon_voices/joel_campbell/?id=5597.

Card, Orson Card. *Ender's Game*. New York: Tor Science Fiction, 1985.

————. *Speaker for the Dead*. New York: Tor Science Fiction, 1986.

Church Educational System. *Church History in the Fullness of Times Student Manual*. Salt Lake City: Church of Jesus Christ of Latter-day Saints, 2003.

Cillizza, Chris. "The Rising: Jon Huntsman, Jr." *Washington Post*, December 9, 2008. Accessed April 1, 2010. http://voices.washingtonpost.com/thefix/the-rising/the-rising-jon-huntsman-jr.html.

Clayton, William. "Come, Come, Ye Saints." In *Hymns of the Church of Jesus Christ of Latter-day Saints*. Salt Lake City: Church of Jesus Christ of Latter-day Saints.

Conger, Kimberly H. "Evangelicals, Issues, and the 2008 Iowa Caucuses." *Politics and Religion* 3 (2010): 130–49.

Cott, Nancy F. *Public Vows: A History of Marriage and the Nation.* Cambridge, Mass.: Harvard University Press, 2000.

Covey, Stephen R. *The Divine Center.* Salt Lake City: Deseret Book, 2005.

———. *The Seven Habits of Highly Effective Families.* New York: St. Martin's Griffin, 1997.

———. *The Seven Habits of Highly Effective People.* New York: Free Press, 2004.

Crawley, Peter. "The Constitution of the State of Deseret." *BYU Studies* 29, no. 4 (1989): 7–22.

Crook, Clive. "The Massachusetts Experiment." *Atlantic,* June 27, 2006. http://www.theatlantic.com/magazine/archive/2006/06/the-massachusetts-experiment/5048/.

Cross, Whitney. *The Burned-over District: The Social and Intellectual History of Enthusiastic Religion in Western New York, 1800–1850.* Ithaca: Cornell University Press, 1950.

Davies, W. D. "Reflections on the Mormon Canon." *Harvard Theological Review* 79, no. 1 (1986): 44–66.

Drehle, David von. "Mad Man: Is Glenn Beck Bad for America?" *Time,* September 17, 2009. Accessed April 1, 2010. http://www.time.com/time/politics/article/0,8599,1924348,00.html.

Driggs, Ken. "After the Manifesto: Modern Polygamy and Fundamentalist Mormons." *Journal of Church and State* 32 (1990): 367–89.

———. "Who Shall Raise the Children? Vera Black and the Rights of Polygamous Utah Parents." *Utah Historical Quarterly* 60 (1992): 27–46.

Dunbar, Willis Frederick, and George S. May. *Michigan: A History of the Wolverine State.* Grand Rapids: Eerdmans, 1995.

Durham, Homer. "A Political Interpretation of Mormon History." *Pacific Historical Review* 13, no. 2 (1994): 136–50.

Dutcher, Richard. "Richard Dutcher: 'Parting Words' on Mormon Movies." *Daily Herald,* April 11, 2007. Accessed April 1, 2010. http://www.heraldextra.com/news/opinion/utah-valley/article_c07f4ae0-bbee-5265-89c1-bae7b12ce676.html.

Ehat, Andrew F. "It Seems Like Heaven Began on Earth: Joseph Smith and the Constitution of the Kingdom of God." *BYU Studies* 20, no. 3 (1980): 253–79.

Eisenach, Eldon J. "Conclusion: Religion, Politics, and American Identity after September 11: Reflections on Recent Scholarship." In *Religion, Politics, and American Identity*, edited by David S. Gutterman and Andrew R. Murphy, 269–91. Lanham, Md.: Lexington Books, 2006.

Eliot, Charles William. "Five American Contributions to Civilization." In *The Oxford Book of American Essays*, edited by Brander Matthews, 208–307. Oxford: Oxford University Press, 1914.

Embry, Jessie L. *Mormon Polygamous Families: Life in the Principle.* Draper, Utah: Greg Kofford Books, 2006.

Evans, Steve. "South Park Mormonism." *Dialogue*, June 3, 2006. Accessed April 1, 2010. http://bycommonconsent.com/2006/06/03/south-park-mormonism.

Fine, Sidney. *Expanding the Frontier of Civil Rights: Michigan, 1948–1968.* Detroit: Wayne State University Press, 2000.

Firmage, Edwin Brown, and Richard Collin Mangrum. *Zion in the Courts: A Legal History of the Church of Jesus Christ of Latter-day Saints, 1830–1900.* Champaign: University of Illinois Press 1988.

Fischer, Claude. *Made in America: A Social History of American Culture and Character.* Chicago: University of Chicago Press, 2010.

Fleming, Stephen J. "Congenial to Almost Every Shade of Radicalism: The Delaware Valley and the Success of Early Mormonism." *Religion and American Culture* 17, no. 2 (2007): 129–64.

Furniss, Noman F. *The Utah Conflict: 1850–1859.* New Haven: Yale University Press, 2005.

Garcia, David Alire. "Senator Tom Udall?" *New Mexico Independent*, May 23, 2008. Accessed August 1, 2010. http://newmexicoindependent.com/1178/senator-tom-udall.

Gellinek, Christian, and Richard Hacken. "Christ in America? Mormonism as a Christian Religion in Comparative Ecclesiastical History." *Brigham Young University Studies* 39, no. 1 (2000): 212–15.

Gilchrist, Brent. *Cultus Americanus: Varieties of the Liberal Tradition in American Political Culture, 1600–1865.* New York: Rowman & Littlefield, 2007.

Givens, Terryl. "The Book of Mormon and Religious Epistemology." *Dialogue* 34, nos. 3–4 (2001): 31–54.

———. *By the Hand of Mormon: The American Scripture that Launched a New World Religion.* Oxford: Oxford University Press, 2002.

———. *The Latter-day Saint Experience in America.* Westport, Conn.: Greenwood Press, 2004.

———. *People of Paradox.* Oxford: Oxford University Press, 2007.

———. *The Viper on the Hearth.* Oxford: Oxford University Press, 1997.

Gordon, Sarah Barringer. *The Mormon Question: Polygamy and Constitutional Conflict in Nineteenth Century America.* Chapel Hill: University of North Carolina Press, 2002.

Gottlieb, Robert, and Peter Wiley. *America's Saints: The Rise of Mormon Power.* New York: Putnam, 1984.

Grossman, Lev. "Stephenie Meyer: A New J. K. Rowling?" *Time*, April 24, 2008. Accessed April 1, 2010. http://www.time.com/time/magazine/article/0,9171,1734838,00.html#ixzz0gT11bdmP.

Hafen, Leroy R., and Ann W. Hafen, eds. *Mormon Resistance: A Documentary Account of the Utah Expedition, 1857–1858.* Lincoln: University of Nebraska Press, 2005.

Haight, David. "He Is Not Here, He Is Risen." *Ensign,* May 1980, 9.

Hanks, Maxine, and Jean Kinney Williams. *Mormon Faith in America.* New York: Facts on File, 2003.

———. *The Village Enlightenment in America: Popular Religion and Science in the Nineteenth Century.* Urbana: University of Illinois Press, 2000.

Hansen, Klaus J. "Joseph Smith and the Political Kingdom of God." *American West* 5 (September 1968): 20–24.

Hardy, Grant. *Understanding the Book of Mormon: A Reader's Guide.* Oxford: Oxford University Press, 2010.

Hardy, Kenneth R. "Social Origins of American Scientists and Scholars." *Science*, August 9, 1974, 497–506.

Hatch, Nathan O. *The Democratization of American Christianity.* New Haven: Yale University Press, 1991.

———. "The Populist View of Joseph Smith." In *Mormons and Mormonism*, edited by E. A. Eliason, 123–36. Urbana: University of Illinois Press, 2001.

Havrilesky, Heather. I Like to Watch. *Salon.com*, March 5, 2006. Accessed April 1, 2010. http://www.salon.com/entertainment/iltw/ 2006/03/05/big_love/index.html.

Hazen, Craig James. *The Village Enlightenment in America: Popular Religion and Science in the Nineteenth Century.* Urbana: University of Illinois Press, 2000.

Hersh, Burton. *The Shadow President: Ted Kennedy in Opposition.* Hanover, N.H.: Steelforth Press, 1997.

Hewitt, Hugh. *Mormon in the White House? Ten Things Every American Should Know about Mitt Romney.* Washington, D.C.: Regnery, 2007.

Hicks, Chris. "TV Portrayal of Mormons Mean, Callous." *Deseret Morning News,* June 5, 2005. Accessed April 1, 2010. http://www .deseretnews.com/article/1,5143,600131613,00.html.

Hill, Marvin S. *Quest for Refuge: The Flight from American Pluralism.* Salt Lake City: Signature Books, 1989.

Hinckley, Gordon, James Faust, and Thomas Monson. *The Family: A Proclamation to the World.* http://www.lds.org/library/display/ 0,4945,161-1-11.

Hinton, Wayne K., and Stephen Roberds. "Public Opinion, Culture, and Religion in Utah." In *Utah in the Twentieth Century,* edited by Brian Q. Cannon and Jessie L. Embry, 227–44. Logan: Utah State University Press, 2009.

Hollinger, David. *The American Intellectual Tradition: A Sourcebook.* 4th ed. 2 vols. Oxford: Oxford University Press, 2001–5.

Howe, Daniel Walker. *What Hath God Wrought: The Transformation of America, 1815–1848.* Oxford: Oxford University Press, 2007.

Jennings, Ken. "Politicians and Pundits, Please Stop Slandering My Mormon Faith." *New York Daily News,* December 18, 2007. Accessed April 1, 2010. http://www.nydailynews.com/ opinions/2007/12/19/2007-12-19_politicians_pundits_ please_stop_slander.html

Johns, Andrew L. "Achilles' Heel: The Vietnam War and George Romney's Bid for the Presidency, 1967 to 1968." *Michigan Historical Review* 26 (2000): 1–29.

Johnson, Frank, and William J. Leffler. *Jews and Mormons: Two Houses of Israel.* Hoboken, N.J.: Ktav, 2000.

Jospe, Raphael, Truman G. Madsen, and Seth Ward, eds. *Covenant and Chosenness in Judaism and Mormonism*. Madison: Fairleigh Dickinson University Press, 2001.

Kennedy, John F. "Address at the Mormon Tabernacle (September 26, 1963)." Miller Center of Public Affairs. Accessed August 1, 2010. http://millercenter.org/scripps/archive/speeches/detail /3378.

Kimball, Spencer. "First Presidency Message: The Gospel Vision of the Arts." *Ensign*, July 1977, 3.

King, Stephen. "Television Impaired." *Entertainment Weekly*, February 1, 2007. Accessed April 1, 2010. http://www.ew.com/ew/article/ 0,,20008933,00.html.

Kohol, Lawrence. *The Politics of Individualism: Parties and the American Character in the Jacksonian Era*. Oxford: Oxford University Press, 1989.

Kouchel, Bernard L. "A Chronicle of the Mormon Baptism of Jewish Holocaust Victims." JewishGen. http://www.jewishgen.org/ infofiles/ldsagree.html.

Krakauer, Jon. *Under the Banner of Heaven*. New York: Random House, 2003.

Lamb, Charles M. *Housing Segregation in Suburban America since 1960: Presidential and Judicial Politics*. Cambridge: Cambridge University Press, 2005.

Leonard, Glen M. "The Mormon Boundary Question in the 1849–1850 Statehood Debates." *Journal of Mormon History* 18, no. 1 (1992): 114–36.

Lillpop, John. "Anti-Mormon Bigotry Tainting Republican Votes?" *Canada Free Press*, February 5, 2008. Accessed April 15, 2010. http://www.canadafreepress.com/index.php/article/1734.

Linker, Damon. "The Big Test: Taking Mormonism Seriously." *New Republic,* January 15, 2007. Accessed August 1, 2010. http:// www.tnr.com/article/politics/the-big-test.

Liu, Melinda. "Mr. Huntsman Goes to Beijing." *Newsweek*, November 16, 2009. Accessed August 15, 2010. http://www.newsweek .com/id/223058.

MacKinnon, William P., ed. *At Sword's Point: A Documentary History of the Utah War to 1858.* Norman: University of Oklahoma Press, 2008.

————. "Loose in the Stacks: A Half-Century with the Utah War and Its Legacy." *Dialogue: A Journal of Mormon Thought* 40, no. 1 (2007): 43–81.

Mahoney, Tom. *The Story of George Romney: Builder, Salesman, Crusader.* New York: Harper and Brothers, 1960.

Marx, Leo. *The Machine in the Garden.* Oxford: Oxford University Press, 2000.

Mason, Robert. *Richard Nixon and the Quest for a New Majority.* Raleigh: University of North Carolina Press, 2004.

Mauss, Armand. *The Angel and the Beehive: The Mormon Struggle with Assimilation.* Champaign: University of Illinois Press, 1994.

McDermott, Gerald. "How Do We Know about Jesus?" In *Claiming Christ*, edited by Robert L. Millet and Gerald R. McDermott, 15–29. Grand Rapids: Brazos Press, 2007.

McFarland, Sheena. "Reid Tells BYU Crowd That Socially Responsible Dems Mirror Mormon Values." *Salt Lake Tribune*, October 9, 2007. Accessed August 15, 2010. http://web.archive.org/web/20071013011413/http://www.sltrib.com/ci_7128071.

McHugh, James T. "A Liberal Theocracy: Philosophy, Theology, and Utah Constitutional Law." *Albany Law Review* 60 (1996–97): 1515–20.

Melton, J. Gordon. *Encyclopedia of American Religions.* 7th ed. Farmington Hills, Mich.: Thomson Gale, 2002.

Meyer, Stephenie. *The Twilight Saga Complete Collection.* Boston: Little, Brown Books for Young Readers, 2010.

Millet, Robert L. *A Different Jesus? The Christ of Latter-day Saints.* Grand Rapids: Eerdmans, 2005.

Millet, Robert L., and Gerald R. McDermott. *Claiming Christ.* Grand Rapids: Brazos Press, 2007.

Mills, Tony-Allen. "News Review Interview: Stephenie Meyer." *Sunday Times*, August 10, 2008. Accessed April 1, 2010. http://entertainment.timesonline.co.uk/tol/arts_and_entertainment/books/article4492238.ece.

Montesquieu. *The Spirit of the Laws.* Cambridge: Cambridge University Press, 1989.

"Mr. Smooth of Massachusetts." *Economist,* July 7, 2007.

Nash, Roderick. *Wilderness and the American Mind.* New Haven: Yale University Press, 1982.

National Party Conventions, 1831–2004. Washington, D.C.: CQ Press, 2005.

Neuhaus, Richard John. "Is Mormonism Christian?" *First Things* (March 2000): 97–115.

Nugent, Walter. *Habits of Empire: A History of American Expansion.* New York: Alfred A. Knopf, 2008.

Orlet, Christopher. "No Mormons Need Apply." *American Spectator,* February 14, 2008. Accessed September 1, 2010. http://spectator. org/archives/2008/02/14/no-mormons-need-apply.

Ostling, Richard, and Joan Ostling. *Mormon America: The Power and Promise.* San Francisco: HarperOne, 1999.

Paley, William. *The Principles of Moral and Political Philosophy.* Boston: Benj. Mussey, 1853.

Parker, Kathleen. "Health Reform, Utah's Way." *Washington Post,* July 24, 2009. Accessed August 1, 2010. http://www.washing tonpost.com/wp-dyn/content/article/2009/07/24/AR200 9072401956.html?sid=ST2009072802120.

Penning, James M. "Americans' Views of Muslims and Mormons: A Social Identity Theory of Approach." *Religion and Politics* 2 (2009): 277–302.

Perry, L. Tom. "God's Hand in the Founding of America." *New Era,* July 1976, 45.

Pew Research Center. "A Portrait of Mormons in the U.S." Pew Forum on Religion and Public Life, July 24, 2009. Accessed April 1, 2010. http://pewforum.org/Christian/Mormon/A-Portrait -of-Mormons-in-the-US.aspx.

————."A Post-Election Look at Religious Voters in the 2008 Elections." Pew Research Forum, December 8, 2008. Accessed April 1, 2010. http://pewforum.org/Politics-and-Elections/ A-Post-Election-Look-at-Religious-Voters-in-the-2008 -Election.aspx.

————. "Public Opinion about Mormons." Pew Research Forum, December 4, 2007. Accessed April 1, 2010. http://pew research.org/pubs/648/romney-mormon.

————. "Public Still Getting to Know Leading GOP Candidates." Pew Research Forum, December 5, 2007. Accessed April 1, 2010. http://pewresearch.org/pubs/651/republican-candidates.

Pillis, M. "The Social Sources of Mormonism." In *American Church History: A Reader,* edited by H. Warner, 346–56. Nashville: Abingdon, 1998.

Poll, Richard Douglas. *The Quixotic Mediator: Thomas L. Kane and the Utah War.* Ogden: Weber State College Press, 1985.

Poniewozik, James. "Top Ten Returning TV Series," *Time,* December 9, 2007. Accessed April 1, 2010. http://www.time.com/time/specials/2007/article/0,28804,1686204_1686244_1691404,00.html.

Porter, Bruce D., and Gerald D. McDermott. "Is Mormonism Christian?" *First Things* (October 2008).

Quinn, Michael D. "The Council of Fifty and Its Members, 1844–1945." *BYU Studies* 20, no. 2 (1980): 163–98.

Remini, Robert. *Joseph Smith.* New York: Viking, 2002.

Resolution Urging Jell-O Recognition. 2001 General Session, State of Utah. Sponsored by Honorable Leonard M. Blackham. Accessed April 15, 2010. http://www.le.state.ut.us/~2001/bills/sbillenr/SR0005.htm.

Reyes, Antonio. "Mormonism, Americanism, and Mexico." *American Behavioral Scientist* 40, no. 7 (1997): 902–13.

Riess, Jana. *What Would Buffy Do? Vampire Slayer as a Spiritual Guide.* Hoboken, N.J.: John Wiley & Sons, 2004.

Robinson, Stephen E. *Are Mormons Christian?* Salt Lake City: Bookcraft, 1998.

Robinson, Timothy. *Turnaround: Crisis, Leadership, and the Olympic Games.* Washington, D.C.: Regnery, 2004.

Roche, Lisa Riley. "Huntsman Calls Self 'Moderating Voice' on Many Issues." *Deseret News,* February 10, 2009. Accessed August 5, 2010. http://www.deseretnews.com/article/1,5143,70528 4093,00.html.

Romney, Mitt, with Timothy Robinson. *Turnaround: Crisis, Leadership, and the Olympic Games*. Washington, D.C.: Regnery, 2004.

Ryan, Maureen. "It's Hard out Here for a Polygamist: 'Big Love.'" *Chicago Tribune*, March 9, 2006. Accessed April 1, 2010. http://features blogs.chicagotribune.com/entertainment_tv/big_love.

Sandoz, Ellis. *A Government of Laws*. Columbia: University of Missouri Press, 2001.

————. *Republicanism, Religion, and the Soul of America*. Columbia: University of Missouri Press, 2006.

Schlesinger, Arthur M., Sr. "Our Ten Contributions to Civilization." *Atlantic*, March 1959, 65–69.

Shipps, Jan. "Is Mormonism Christian? Reflections on a Complicated Question." In *Mormons and Mormonism: An Introduction to an American World Religion*, edited by Eric A. Eliason, 76–97. Urbana: University of Illinois Press, 2001.

————. *Mormonism: The Story of a New Religious Tradition*. Urbana: University of Illinois Press, 1984.

————. *Sojourner in the Promised Land: Forty Years among the Mormons*. Urbana: University of Illinois Press, 2000.

Smart, Tom. *In Plain Sight: The Startling Truth behind the Elizabeth Smart Investigation*. Chicago: Chicago Review Press, 2005.

Smith, Joseph. *The Book of Mormon: Another Testament of Jesus Christ*. Salt Lake City: Church of Latter Day Saints, 1981.

————. *The Doctrine and Covenants of the Church of Jesus Christ of Latter-day Saints*. Carlisle, Mass.: Applewood Books, 2009.

————. *History of the Church of Jesus Christ of Latter-day Saints*. 7 vols. Salt Lake City: Deseret Book, 1978.

————. *Teachings of the Prophet Joseph Smith*. Ed. Joseph F. Smith Jr. Salt Lake City: Deseret News Press, 1965.

Snow, Tyson. "Sen. Reid Explains Mormonism and Liberal Agenda." *Universe*, February 24, 2001. Accessed August 15, 2010. http://newsnet.byu.edu/story.cfm/13779.

Stewart, Amy K. "BYU Center to Develop Animation Creations." *Deseret News*, March 28, 2008. Accessed April 1, 2010. http://www.deseretnews.com/article/1,5143,695265400,00.html.

Sullivan, Amy. "Mitt Romney's Evangelical Problem." *Washington Monthly*, September 2005. Accessed August 15, 2010. http://www.washingtonmonthly.com/features/2005/0509.sullivan1.html.

Talmage, James E. *Jesus the Christ*. Salt Lake City: Deseret Book, 1982.

Taylor, John. *The Gospel Kingdom. Salt Lake City:* Deseret Book, 1943

Thomas, Ethan. "'Twilight' Loses Luster with Deseret Book." *Deseret News*, April 23, 2009. Accessed April 1, 2010. http://www.deseretnews.com/article/705299108/Twilight-loses-luster-with-Deseret-Book.html.

Thorndike, E. L. "The Origins of Superior Men." *Scientific Monthly*, May 1943, 424–32.

Tocqueville, Alexis de. *Democracy in America*. Translated by Harvey Mansfield and Debra Winthrop. Chicago: University of Chicago Press, 2002.

Underwood, Grant. "Mormons and the Millennial World-View." In *Mormon Identities in Transition,* edited by Douglas J. Davies. New York: Cassell, 1996.

Van Wagoner, Richard S. *Mormon Polygamy: A History*. Salt Lake City: Signature Books, 1989.

Wall, Elissa, and Lisa Pulitzer. *Stolen Innocence: My Story of Growing up in a Polygamous Sect, Becoming a Teenage Bride, and Breaking Free of Warren Jeffs*. New York: HarperCollins, 2008.

Watson, Harry L. *Liberty and Power: The Politics of Jacksonian America*. New York: Hill and Wang, 2006.

Wegner, Frederick L. "Living a Jewish Life in Utah Society." In *God and Country: Politics in Utah*, edited by Jeffery E. Sells, 319–24. Salt Lake City: Signature Books, 2005.

White, O. Kendall. "Mormonism in America and Canada: Accommodation to Nation-State." *Canadian Journal of Sociology–Cahiers Canadiens de Sociologie* 3, no. 2 (1978): 161–81.

White, Theodore H. *The Making of the President, 1968*. New York: Atheneum, 1969.

Wicks, Robert S., and Fred R. Foister. *Presidential Politics and the Assassination of the First Mormon Prophet*. Logan: Utah State University Press, 2005.

Widstoe, John A. *Evidences and Reconciliations*. Salt Lake City: Bookcraft, 1960.

Williams, Florence. "The Coyote Caucus Takes the West to Washington." *High Country News*, October 11, 2004. Accessed April 1, 2010. http://www.hcn.org/issues/284/15040.

Wilson, Ben. "LDS Church Rejects Polygamous Accusations." *Deseret News*, February 28, 2006. Accessed April 1, 2010. http://www.deseretnews.com/article/1,5143,635188091,00.html.

Winder, Michael Kent. *Presidents and Prophets: The Story of America's Presidents and the LDS Church*. American Fork, Utah: Covenant Communications, 2007.

Winston, Diane. "Back to the Future: Religion, Politics, and the Media." *American Quarterly* 59, no. 3 (2007): 969–89.

Witcover, Jules. *Marathon: The Pursuit of the Presidency, 1972–1976*. New York: Viking Press, 1977.

Woods, Fred E. *A Gamble in the Desert: The Mission in Las Vegas (1855–57)*. Salt Lake City: Mormon Historic Sites Foundation, 2005.

Wright, N. T. *What Saint Paul Really Said*. Grand Rapids: Eerdmans, 1997.

Yates, Thomas. "Count Tolstoi and 'The American Religion.'" *Improvement Era* 42 (1939): 94.

Yorgason, Ethan R. *Transformation of the Mormon Culture Region*. Champaign: University of Illinois Press, 2003.

INDEX

CPSIA information can be obtained
at www.ICGtesting.com
Printed in the USA
LVHW11s2230250918
591330LV00001B/64/P